THE STORY OF JOB

James Yeager

ISBN 979-8-88685-169-4 (paperback)
ISBN 979-8-88685-170-0 (digital)

Christian Faith Publishing
832 Park Avenue
Meadville, PA 16335
www.christianfaithpublishing.com

Printed in the United States of America

Dedicated to all the great movie directors of our time, both living and deceased, including: Robert Aldrich, Robert Altman, Hideaki Anno, Jack Arnold, Yashimitsu Banno, Laslo Benedek, Ingmar Bergman, John Boorman, Tim Burton, John Carpenter, William Castle, Michael Cimino, Kevin Connor, Merian C. Cooper, Francis Ford Coppola, Roger Corman, Wes Craven, Joe Dante, Leonardo Deflippis, Cecil B. DeMille, Brian DePalma, Vittorio DeSica, Michael Dougherty, Gareth Edwards, Federico Fellini, Richard Fleischer, John Ford, William Friedkin, Jun Fukuda, William Girdler, Bert I. Gordon, John Guillermin, Koji Hashimoto, Bryon Haskin, Howard Hawks, Shinji Higuchi, George Roy Hill, Alfred Hitchcock, Ishiro Honda, Hiroshi Inagaki, Peter Jackson, Nathan Juran, Shusuke Kaneko, Koichi Kawakita, Elia Kazan, Teinosuke Kinugasa, Ryuhei Kitamura, Stanley Kramer, Stanley Kubrick, Kunio Kunisada, Akira Kurosawa, David Lean, Sergio Leone, Eugene Lourie, George Lucas, Steve Miner, Kazui Nihonmatsu, Haruyasu Noguchi, Christian Nyby, Motoyoshi Oda, Takao Okawara, Kenjiro Omori, Pier Paolo Pasolini, Sam Peckinpaw, Sidney Pink, Roman Polanski, Sidney Pollack, Nicholas Ray, Jordan V. Roberts, George A. Romero, Roberto Rossellini, Martin Scorsese, Ridley Scott, Koji Shima, Ernest B. Shoedsack, M. Night Shyamalan, Steven Spielberg, George Stevens, Oliver Stone, Shigeo Tanaka, Ryuta Tasaki, Masaaki Tezuka, J Lee Thompson, Jacques Tourneur, Eiji Tsuburaya, King Vidor, Billy Wilder, Robert Wise, William Wyler, Kensho Yamashito, Tetsuya Yamauchi, Noriaki Yuasa, Franco Zeffirelli—just to name a few.

A man who is born of woman is of few days and full of trouble. He cometh forth like a flower and is cut down; he fadeth also like a shadow and continueth not.

—Job 14:1–2

And Holy Scripture says: In the Old Testament, somewhere between 600–1,000 BC, Satan, the accuser, prince of darkness, father of all lies and whom, centuries later, Jesus Christ would call "a murderer," appealed to God, asking, "Is it for nothing that your servant Job is God-fearing?"

On that very same day, all the servants of God and members of the divine council gathered together and were assembling before the Lord God in the heavens, presenting themselves before him, bowing to him, and offering him praise and worship. All of paradise was filled with the harmonious sounds of the choirs of heaven, singing praise and worship to God. The Lord God looked out at it all and saw it was good and was most pleased. The Lord looked at Satan who was still standing among the others. The Lord said to Satan, "Where have you been?"

Satan then replied to the Lord, saying, "Roaming the earth and prowling among its inhabitants, seeking the ruin of souls."

The Lord asked Satan, "From your question, I take it you have noticed my servant, Job? There is no one on earth like him, blameless and upright, fearing God and avoiding evil!"

Then Satan again answered the Lord, asking, "Again, I ask, is it for nothing that Job is God-fearing? Have you not surrounded him and his family and all that he owns and treasures with your protection? Have you not blessed the work of his hands over and over again, one hundredfold, as well as his livestock that are spread over the vast land that he owns? But now put forth your hand and touch all that he has and put it to ruin and, surely, he will curse you to your face."

Then the Lord God said to Satan, "Very well, be it, for now, as you will, all that he has is in your power. But remember one very stern command: You are not to lay a single hand on him! You are not to do him harm nor injure him in any way! Now be off!"

So Satan went forth from the presence of the Lord to the presence of those among the earth.

Now, on earth, in the land of Uz, there lived the blameless and upright man named Job, who feared God and avoided evil. He lived with his wife, Sitidos, in a beautiful and vast mansion made of stone and marble, which sat on a rocky hill, overlooking all of his land. Before the front entrance, which was adorned and supported by five marble pillars, was a stone terrace. Beyond the terrace was a sharp cliff leading to an enormous and very deep lake, which led to the sea at about 250 meters below. Seven sons and three daughters were born to Job through his wife, Sitidos. He had seven thousand sheep and was rich with cattle—three thousand camels, five hundred yoke of oxen, five hundred she-donkeys, and a very large household in the mansion—all making him the wealthiest of men and greater than anyone in the east. His sons would take turns giving feasts and sending invitations to their three sisters to come and eat and drink with them.

One evening, just before sunset, Job and Sitidos were walking on a windswept mountainside, under a sapphire blue sky. He embraced her, kissed her lips, and said, "It's such a beautiful evening!"

She replied, while gently pushing him away, "I can't now. It's getting late, and I have to gather herbs for the stew tonight."

He said, "Stew! Don't forget about the feast we are having tomorrow night here with the children. They are all coming this time. I have a list of things for you to gather for it."

She said, "All right, I'm not a magician, you know!"

As she walked away, he looked up to the sky and said, "I thank you, Lord, for all you've given me. What did I do that all this fortune from you has come to me? How have I ever begotten such blessings from you? I thank you, again, oh great Yahweh, forever and a day. Amen!"

The next evening, after the feast, Job and his entire family were in the mansion, talking, laughing, and singing psalms of praise and thanksgiving to God. Job had his servants clear the dirty dishes then took his family into the parlor. He stretched out his arms over his sons' heads and prayed, "Yahweh, forgive them any sins they may have committed. Have mercy on them, and please remember, they have only sinned out of human weakness and not out of malice."

Sitidos sighed and rolled her eyes, then said, "We have good sons. Look at all they do for their parents and sisters. What sins could they have ever committed?"

Job said, "No one knows what is in the heart of God."

Later that evening after dark, when everything was cleaned up, Job dismissed his servants, sent all his sons and daughters back to their own homes, and sent his wife to bed. He himself went outside and walked up to a pile of seven freshly slaughtered lambs. He then proceeded to lay each one on a separate pile of wood and lit fire to each one with a lit torch. As the fires all blazed brightly and the smoke disappeared into the darkness of night, he knelt down, holding the lit torch in his right hand over his head, looked up to the heavens and, again, prayed, "Oh great Yahweh, you well know this is now the twentieth time I've made these burnt offerings in atonement for my sins and for the sins of my wife, seven sons, and three daughters. Forgive us, Almighty, for it might be that my children have sinned and cursed you in their hearts."

After each dead lamb's flesh and bones were completely consumed by the burning flames, Job allowed each fire to burn until it was no more than smoldering embers. He then gathered all the ashes from the dead animals, placed them in a jar, and threw them into the lake and again offered prayers and alms to Yahweh. He then retired to the mansion and went to bed.

The next morning, just before daybreak, Job and Sitidos were sound asleep in bed when Job suddenly woke up abruptly, sat up in bed, and nervously looked around. He was all sweaty and trembling in fear while looking around as if sensing ominous danger. Outside, a mob of about fifty petty thieves and bandits were riding in from the countryside on horseback, then stopped at the shore of the lake and were looking up at the mansion on the rocky hillside. The mob's leader, Zerah, and a few others, jumped off of their horses, onto the ground while holding in their hands, lit torches for light. They squatted down on the lakeshore and were looking up at the mansion.

At this time, Satan entered Zerah's body and took possession of it. They kept gazing up, puzzled while trying to concoct a plan to break in and get past the four armed guards whom they were watching walk back and forth, in front of the main entrance. Zerah turned to his right and said to his leading henchman, "I can't believe he only has four guards way out here in this wilderness with such a huge mansion." He laughed and said, "Anyway, it should be pretty easy, all of us taking down only four guards."

The henchman said, "Job is a man of faith. He relies only on his invisible and imaginary God for help. But after this night, we'll make him believe there is no God."

Zerah sent several of his henchmen up to the palace to investigate. They rode around the left side of the lake, then up a long flight of stone steps to the entrance and saw it was all clear. Since it was nearly daybreak, the guards left their posts. The bandits motioned to Zerah and the others below to come. They all rode as fast as they could around the left side of the lake, then around the north end of the castle to the left and up the mountain. The guards turned around and saw the mob of bandits on horseback, holding flaming torches and riding as fast as they could toward them. The bandits rode up to the entrance and proceeded to raid the castle.

They commenced to throw lit torches against the door. With their swords, they went slashing through the front lawn, pushing over tables and chairs, scattering many silver and gold dishes and vases on the ground, and smashing them underfoot. They killed two of the guards by slicing their throats with a sword as blood flew into the air. One bandit rode past yet another guard and, on horseback, reached down with a sword and not only sliced his throat but cut his head clean off. They threw their lit torches into the trees around the castle, and they all went up in flames. They lit fire to the grass around the castle as more flames rose high into the air. Four bandits rode into the melee, all one after another, holding a huge long chunk of marble, and smashed it into the door. They smashed into it again and again. Then with one last shove, at full force, the bandits broke through the door as it broke in half and fell forward into the vestibule.

The bandits all ran in, some on their horses, swinging their swords and smashing Job's most prized possessions. One bandit swung his sword with full force into a glass case and smashed it to pieces. Hundreds of pieces of jewelry fell out and scattered onto the floor. Also, many priceless gems and stones were trampled into the floor under the horses' feet. Some of them even put on rings, necklaces, and bracelets and were singing, laughing, and dancing around in mock rituals and ceremonies. They went on swinging their swords through the air in a wild frenzy, vandalizing the whole downstairs.

The fourth palace guard ran in and lifted a spear in his right hand, ready to throw it at the leader—Zerah. But one of the savage horsemen immediately raised his sword in his right hand and heaved it full force at the guard, driving it straight into his chest. A stream of blood flowed out of his chest as the guard screamed, dropped his spear, and grabbed hold of the sword in his chest. He pulled at it, then fell backward, knocking over a piece of furniture. The bandits then proceeded to light the curtains, furniture, and even the walls and blinds on fire with their lit torches, charring them black; and to torch the entire parlor room, dining area, and kitchen, setting them all ablaze.

Job and Sitidos ran down the stairs and into the parlor room. They were screaming, coughing, and choking from the smoke and flames while trying to get through to the vestibule where they could see there was no fire. With a powerful swing of his arm, Zerah, from behind, sliced Job's back with his sword, tearing his robe, and causing a deep bloody gash underneath it. Job screamed as the pain went through his entire body, then fell on his right side. Sitidos helped him up to his knees. Job and Sitidos looked up and saw Zerah flying through the air in the middle of the blazing room, straight for them, screaming, "I'll kill you!" with a bloodred face and his sword in his right hand.

At that very moment, Job saw a piece of curtain half-engulfed in fire, lying on the floor. Immediately, he lifted it up with a wooden leg from a piece of furniture and heaved the half that was on fire, right in Zerah's face. Zerah screamed in pain and dropped his sword onto the floor and fell right into a pillar of fire. He screamed and wailed out loud again at the top of his lungs. But with the flaming curtain now on the other side of them, Job and Sitidos now had room to escape.

They held tight to each other, ran out of the flaming parlor room, into the vestibule, and outside into the fresh air, coughing and gagging from the smoke and heat. They were leaning against a stone wall, trying to regain their senses while looking down at the lake and shore many meters below them. They heard an ear-piercing scream from inside the palace, then turned and looked. Running out of the door, directly toward them, was Zerah, his entire body being consumed by one gigantic flame. Zerah leaped up onto the wall, looked down at Job, and screamed loudly in a very low and bloodcurdling voice, "I'll get you for this, you petty little man! I'll surely kill you!" Zerah then stretched out his arms, which were still blazing with fire, and threw himself down over the wall, toward the lake below.

Job and Sitidos looked down but saw no sign of his body, just the shore and lake. They turned and looked at each other in astonishment and horror. They turned again toward the palace and watched as the savages continued their orgy of vandalism. While torching more of the inside of the palace, two of the bandits noticed Job and Sitidos outside. They ran out after them with swords, lit torches, and clubs. Job and Sitidos turned and ran as fast as they could, down the long flight of stone steps. When they got to the bottom, they ran across the shore, toward the lake where they saw several of their servants and maids getting into a rowboat. Job and Sitidos, with about six others, all jumped into the boat and began to row out on to the lake.

They rowed their way about halfway out toward the other shore, looked back, and saw their castle burning in flames with pillars of smoke pouring out of the windows. Job said, "I saw it many times from this spot but never like this."

Sitidos turned to Job and said, "All our lives, we did good. We shared our wealth with others who were less fortunate and did what the Lord, Yahweh, wanted us to do. We were always good and upright in his eyes and in the eyes of others. And now he allows this to happen to us at the hands of these dogs! Now swear eternal vengeance upon them that they may all die a very painful torturous and humiliating death like they are subjecting us to! And curse God and abandon your worship of him!"

But Job just looked back at the castle and said nothing in reply. He watched as more smoke and fire poured out of it, and the trees around it were all crackling, falling over and being consumed by the flames.

One of the servants pointed and said, "What's that in the water?"

In a certain spot in the lake, water was spraying high up into the air like a fountain. They watched the disturbance continue as more water sprayed up into the air. Then it began heading straight for them. Between the shore of the burning castle and the rowboat, the disturbance continued more violently as it traveled very quickly and approached them. Then it suddenly stopped. Then a whirlpool began to churn in the middle of the lake. From the center of it rose a huge fountain of water, then a blinding flash of light streaked from it. Then another flash of light streaked from the same spot. Then, from the center of the whirlpool, a gigantic pillar of fire suddenly shot up high into the air, nearly touching the stars. Then it suddenly disappeared.

Then a gigantic upsurge of water rose from that very spot. Then the upsurge fell back down into the water, revealing a gigantic blue and green dragon-monster covered with yellow scales. It had a long serpent-like neck surmounted by a dragon-like head with five horns, all protruding from the top and two sides of it. The neck was very stout, long, and powerful. The underside of it was ribbed from top to bottom with a long row of red circular scales, and the body was more enormous and massive than any animal they had ever seen. A long tail, which looked like it could reach to the shore, sprung up behind the beast, then fell back down into the water, creating a tremendous splash from both sides of it. It let out of its mouth a high-pitched roar so loud it nearly broke the rowers' eardrums and caused them to squeeze their hands against their ears as hard as they could.

With one tremendous push, it heaved its entire body through the water. Again, it roared and went plowing through the turbulent water, heading right for the boat. It shot out a streak of blazing orange and red fire from its mouth, then shot out a second streak of fire while smoke poured out after each blast, and its eyes turned bright red as lights blazed from them. Job gasped then screamed, "OH MY GOD! It's the monster of chaos and confusion! The Leviathan!"

As it kept approaching the boat, it breathed out of its mouth, in a sudden burst, a blazing red flash of light, then smoke poured from both of its nostrils. Then it snarled at them, showing its enormous dagger-like teeth, each well over six inches long. Again, with a tremendous splash of water, it plunged face first back down into the water and swam as fast as it could toward the boat. Everyone in it screamed in terror. It rose up, right alongside the boat as more water was thrown into the air, hitting the boat and turning it over. All the people were thrown off of it and into the water. They all came back up to the surface and, again, screamed in horror.

The beast, again, opened its mouth, let out an ear-piercing roar, bent down, scooped up the six servants into its mouth, chewed them up, and swallowed them. Job and Sitidos climbed up onto the underside of the boat and saw blood running out of both sides of the dragon's mouth. They looked up and saw the dragon's head coming closer and closer. It opened its mouth right in front of them. After a roar of thunder, the same low, bloodcurdling voice that came from Zerah came from the dragon, saying, "I told you I'd kill you! Now your time has come just like the others!"

Job and Sitidos both screamed, "Get away!"

While the dawn's light began to break, Job and Sitidos saw, in the midst of all the confusion and horror, the full sun rising just above a mountain in the east. Once again, the dragon opened its jaws wide and plunged itself down toward Job and Sitidos. Both closed their eyes, screamed, and held on tight to each other while being doused by torrents of water. Then everyone noticed it got pitch-dark again. Everyone heard a loud screeching caw coming from the east. In a second, Job and Sitidos opened their eyes and looked in that direction. They saw a gigantic bird-like griffin with the body, tail, and legs of a lion and the head, neck, and wings of an eagle, standing on the mountain, right in front of the rising sun, unfurling its wings and blocking out the sunlight. Everyone could only see by the bandits' lit torches on both shores of the lake.

With one powerful flap of its wings, the bird shot high into the sky, then directly down at its full speed, toward the boat. Job said to Sitidos, "Look! It's the great Ziz!"

As the Leviathan lurched further down and opened its mouth wider to devour Job and Sitidos, the Ziz screeched again to draw its attention away from them. The Ziz opened its mouth, and from it came a beautiful trans-like melodious hymn, and everyone fell transfixed on it, including Leviathan. Leviathan rose up and turned around, just as the Ziz straightened its body to an upright position and dropped down, feet first, and, with one tremendous thrust, slashed the right side of Leviathan's face with its talons and then shot upward over its head. Then Leviathan screamed and roared in pain and agony as two streams of blood gushed forward from its face and into the water below. The Ziz swooped down again and grabbed Job and Sitidos in its talons and flew them over the Leviathan's head.

The bandits all watched as the Ziz flew over the castle. But the Leviathan continued swinging its head from side to side as blood was flying in all different directions. While roaring and screaming, Leviathan plunged back down under the water. The surface of the water turned crimson red and was churning violently as Leviathan swam under. Then it calmed.

The next day, Satan was called before God. He was kneeling before him in the meticulously beautiful heavens high above the earth, face down, at the Lord's feet. God was holding his right hand up, high over his head, ready to finally slay Satan. In his mighty wrath, the Lord God shouted at Satan, asking, "Where have you been?"

Then Satan answered the Lord, saying, "I've been roaming and prowling the earth, seeking the ruin of souls."

The Lord God said to Satan, "It was I who sent the mighty Ziz to save Job and his wife in that one brief second in which you would have devoured them. You have disobeyed me, and I shall punish you for it. I shall send a messenger to Job as a punishment against you to confound your campaign against him. You tried to kill him several times—in the burning castle and by possessing Leviathan's body! Yes, you tried to kill him, and I told you that you couldn't. You have disobeyed me, and this shall be your punishment for it! Now away, Satan! On your way!"

Again, Satan left the presence of the Lord and all those in paradise and returned to the presence of those on earth.

Late that afternoon, toward evening, Job was walking in the mountains through ankle-high grass, going to the temple where he and his family went to worship. Still trembling and in tears from the horrible ordeal of the previous night, he was going to talk to his friend, Old Aram, the head rabbi of the temple, and tell him all about what had happened to him and his wife. Satan was still watching him from behind a large tree trunk, again, through the body of Zerah who had a scar on the right side of his face. As Job walked past the tree, Zerah pulled his body behind it to hide. Then, as Job turned right and continued to walk directly toward the temple, Zerah walked out from behind the tree and watched Job, from behind in a clearing, approach the temple. Satan left the body of Zerah and went down toward the ground and beneath a large rock. Zerah fell forward onto the ground, and out from under the rock slithered a very large and deadly green and yellow asp, which shot off at its top speed in the deep grass and followed Job toward the temple. It was keeping up with him, directly behind his heels but never striking at him.

Job opened the door of the temple and walked down a very long hallway until he came to a table and bench in a small lounge area. He hollered twice, "Aram! Aram! Are you here?"

Aram walked out from behind a door, which led to the main temple area, and faced Job directly. The rabbi was an old man sporting a long white beard, shoulder-length hair, was hunched over forward from age, talked with a raspy voice, and had blue veins protruding from the backs of his hands. Job sat down on the bench, facing Aram from across the table, put his head down, held his face in his hands, and began to weep bitterly, saying, "I must tell you everything that happened to me and my wife over the course of this last day."

Aram responded, "You don't have to tell me. I know. It's all over. Everyone is talking about it."

Still crying, Job shouted, "Why me? Why me who always did good and right?"

Aram responded, "First of all, you shouldn't say those words. It's like you are putting yourself above others."

Job said, "But still, why did this all have to happen to me? Why?"

Aram again responded, saying, "It was just one of those things that was Yahweh's will, at least for now. I know it's very hard, but you must accept it and pray to him for justice and vindication."

Job shouted out in sobs, asking, "But I have nothing now! How could a kind and loving God who loves justice allow such a thing to happen? I have nothing now!"

Aram answered, "You may have lost your home and all your assets, but you still have your wife and family, your faith, and me as a friend! And most of all, you still have Yahweh, who I'm sure will do you justice if you only keep praying to him and have faith that he will vindicate you!"

As Job kept crying, Aram got up, turned his back toward him, and poured both of them a cup of hot tea. Aram sat down at the table opposite Job, facing him, and slid the cup over to him and said, "Here, drink this. You'll feel better. I'm sorry, but I've told you all I could. I have no real answers for you. No one does. We don't know the mind of God! But you can come to me anytime and talk. I am your best friend. And you and your wife are more than welcome to stay here with me as long as you want. But I just know that God will someday, somehow, fix all this for you."

Job said, "Thank you. I wish I had your faith."

Aram said, "I think you do."

Aram leaned over forward, folded his hands on the table with the backs of them facing Job, and was going to tell him something very important. Just then, in a few seconds, the asp slithered its way up on to the bench at Job's left side without him seeing it, then up onto the table and raised its head into the air. Aram looked at it and screamed. The asp immediately threw its head forward, struck the back of Aram's right hand with its fangs, then turned around, hissed, and slid back down onto the floor. Job turned to his left and saw it slithering toward the doorway. He got up, ran around the table, and grabbed Aram and held him in his arms. Aram was crying and screaming. In pain, he shouted out, "My God! Job! Job! My dear friend! Help me! It hurts! I'm dying!"

Job screamed, "No! No! Aram! Don't die! Don't die! Please don't die! You can't leave me like this! Please don't die!" Job kept screaming these same words over and over again and pressed his left cheek onto Aram's as Aram kept crying and screaming in pain.

Aram then began to go into violent convulsions as tears were streaming down his face, and he kept screaming and crying. Job saw his right hand was all black and swollen into a distorted ball with the fingers all looking like tiny stubs protruding from it. Now Aram became quieter and calmer. Job let him go slowly onto his back on the floor, then released him.

Aram said to Job in a quivering, weak, and dying voice, "I have been poisoned not by an asp but by Satan, and just as I was going to tell you something of the utmost importance to you and give you something that will save you, save your life someday, and give you more confidence than you could ever imagine. But that's OKAY. Just have faith! Yahweh will keep me alive long enough to give it to you. I know he will. Otherwise, he would not have sent you to me today. It is his plan to help you and, likewise, his sworn punishment to Satan for disobeying him. Reach into my right pocket."

As Job got up and turned around to do so, he saw the asp lying on the floor in front of the doorway, curled up several inches off of the ground with its head in the air, and lashing out its tongue. But Job turned back around and reached in Aram's pocket and pulled out a small piece of parchment. Aram told Job, "I am the messenger God sent to you. Last night, the great Ziz that slashed the Leviathan and saved you and your wife was sent to you from God to save your life from Satan. The Leviathan was Satan in the form of a giant dragon. As you saw, the Ziz slashed the Leviathan's face. And it caused a huge permanent scar on the right side of it. As long as he torments and pursues you, Satan will always carry this scar on the right side of his face. Whether he takes the form of an animal or human, he will always bear this scar. This is how you will know it is him. And you can avoid him. This is Gods' punishment to him.

"And I know you don't understand this now, but someday, you will. That small piece of very old parchment contains a prayer to Mikhael, God's archangel, who once defeated Satan and all of his armies and cast them into the depths of hell. Centuries from now, it will be recited by members of what will then be called the Universal Church. That the promised one of God whom we still await for, will found. Say this prayer in the most vital time of your life to call on Mikhael, and he will come and save you and finally bring you God's peace. You have a lot to endure, my friend, but you will be all right in the end."

Job felt a presence behind him. He turned around as Aram lifted his head and looked too. The asp was not at the doorway anymore, but instead, Zerah was standing in the exact same place, and Job noticed the fresh scar on the right side of his face. Then Zerah's eyes each turned into bright red lights of fire in their sockets and spun backward into his head. He let out a very loud, deafening, and evil laugh. Job turned and looked down at Aram, then back around toward Zerah. But no one nor anything was there, only the long doorway leading to the outside. Again, Job turned and looked down at Aram and watched him close his eyes and lay his head back onto the floor, and Job felt all the life going out of his body. Job said, "Thank you, Aram. I will do all that you told me to do from God." He looked up and prayed, "God bless his soul." Job sunk his face into Aram's chest and cried and wept from deep inside.

Later that evening before sundown, Aram was buried in a mountainside near the temple. After the younger rabbi said the final prayers, all of Aram's family and friends and the congregation of the temple withdrew and went home while mourning and weeping. But Job and Sitidos stayed behind, still weeping and kneeling on the ground, alongside the grave. Sitidos rose up, rubbed Job's shoulders, and said, "Come on. Let's go. There is nothing more we can do here."

Job stood up and said, "Why did this have to happen to him? It's all my fault!"

Sitidos replied, "You mustn't talk like that. You didn't know. You just went to him as a friend, and he knew that. Now let's go."

As they were turning to leave, one of their messengers ran up to them and said, "Job! Job! Sitidos! There is more terrible news about your home and family! All of your children were eating and drinking wine in the house of your eldest son. As they were all having a quiet dinner, the hired hands were outside, driving the oxen who were plowing the fields." As the messenger spoke, he was picturing the events over again in his mind. "The donkeys were grazing quietly beside the oxen. Then the Sabeans from southern Arabia came riding down the mountains from the southwest. They kept riding in closer at full speed, kicking up dirt and dust, then suddenly stopped at only a few hundred meters away. They all formed a long straight horizontal line on their horses and sat there for several moments, watching and stalking us. I counted over one hundred of them.

"The one in the center of the line lifted his arms and head and blew the sound of a war cry into the air, through a horn. They immediately charged at us at full speed on their horses. They raided the entire plantation, trampled the freshly plowed fields under their horses' feet. As they rode in closer, they extended their arms out to the sides, holding swords, and went slicing all of the servants' heads off, spilling their blood. They did this until not one servant was alive. As they rode around in a frenzy, they all began to blow the same war cry into the air and were snapping whips, scaring the oxen who all began to run away. They all drove their horses up behind the oxen, blowing horns, snapping whips, and pushing all of them off of the land and scattering them all into the hills and wilderness. The oxen all fled, many of them pulling the plows right along with them.

"The Sabeans then lit torches and set fire to the plantation, burning the land and setting fire to all the sheds and stables and servants' houses. Finally, the Sabeans rode up to the castle, broke the doors down, and as the bandits did before them, began to raid it. Many jumped off of their horses and went running through the entire castle, smashing everything to bits all of your valuable possessions that the bandits were hording for themselves. Inside, the Sabeans were chasing the bandits while stabbing them, slicing their heads off, and pushing them out of windows and through the doors. Outside, the Sabeans continued riding all around the castle on their horses, killing the bandits, trampling them under the feet of their horses, and pushing them off the tall cliffs. They chased all the bandits to the edge of the cliff and pushed them all down, onto the rocks, and even into the water for the Leviathan to devour. Then they went back inside of the castle and took possession of it. I alone have escaped to tell you."

He was still speaking when another messenger came and said, "Just as this raid was finally over, we saw the Chaldeans from southern Mesopotamia and Babylonia, riding down from the mountains as well. There had to have been hundreds of them on horseback. They all divided up and formed three columns of armies behind each other. Some servants said they had counted a hundred. Some said they counted two hundred. Still others said they counted 250 or 300. I counted 340. And there probably were more. The soldier in the middle of the front column put his two middle fingers in his mouth and let out a very high-pitched whistle. They all charged full speed ahead. They, likewise, rode past the servants, slicing their heads off, spilling their blood all over the ground, and stabbing and killing them mercilessly. They, too, set fire to the ground, torched the trees, and went riding violently behind camels, throwing lit torches at them, snapping whips, and driving them all off the land, and scattering them into the wilderness. They lit fire to a barn and to the last of the stables. All the horses came thundering out in a panic and ran as fast as they could into the wilderness and up into the mountains. They killed the rest of the servants and drove the remaining camels off of the plantation.

"They, too, rode up to the castle, and one of the Chaldeans pulled his horse up on to its hind legs. As it dropped back down, it broke the castle doors in with its two front feet. The Chaldeans rode through the castle and began killing all the Sabeans from their horses with swords and spears. They vandalized the entire inside of the castle and destroyed everything that the Sabeans owned and treasured. With the force of an army, these Chaldeans thrust all of the Sabeans out of the castle and pushed them over the cliff and down into the water for the Leviathan to devour. But most of the Sabeans escaped onto their horses. They all fled, running away on horseback, fleeing from the Chaldeans who chased them many miles into the countryside. The Chaldeans watched the last of the Sabeans disappear into the horizon beyond the desert. Then they returned to the castle and took full possession of it. I alone have escaped to tell you!"

He was still speaking when another messenger came and said, "Your sons and daughters were eating and drinking wine in the house of their eldest brother. Suddenly a great wind came from across the desert and turned into a violent wind storm. As it spun like a whirlwind, it then commenced to tear up everything in its path. It spread dirt and dust for miles and ruined crops and carried poisonous pollens with it, which killed all the cattle and plagued the entire area. Then the funnel of wind sped toward the house of your eldest son. It broke the door down and spread through the entire house. An extremely violent wind blew through the house, sending tables and chairs crashing into the walls while your children were all screaming and going into hysterics. The wind smashed the four corners of the house. It collapsed upon the young people, killing them all. I alone have escaped to tell you!"

He was still speaking when another messenger came and said, "God's fire has risen from the water and has fallen from the heavens! A large pillar of fire shot up out of the lake, high into the air. It struck a cloud and rained fire down toward the earth. It struck the sheep and servants and consumed them. As this was happening, we were all horrified as we could hear their screams and wails of pain and agony. The fire set the entire ground ablaze! A gigantic column of water was thrown high into the air from the lake, and a streak of blinding red light flashed from it. As it rained back down, the dreaded Leviathan, the monster of chaos and confusion, emerged from it. It let out a roar and scream of defiance against God and man and walked out on to the land. It continued roaring its deafening cry into the air as it went on, trampling the fields and plantations, ruining the land, and crushing the supply huts and houses into the ground.

"With another mighty and deafening roar, it breathed out of its mouth a gigantic red flame onto the ground, setting it all on fire, and burning it to a crisp. It breathed its deadly fire again, this time straight ahead, and torched the mountains, lighting them on fire. The fires blazed uncontrollably high into the air. As it turned its body, its long powerful tail struck and toppled an entire row of red wood trees. It roared again and galloped forward, crushing more of the huts and barns, driving them into the ground and smashing still more of them with its enormous tail. Its huge feet continuously pounded the ground as it ran, smashing the rest of the huts and small farm buildings to splinters. It pushed its massive body into a huge forest of trees, again, hurdling them all to the ground.

"Again it roared and exhaled from its mouth its flaming breath and set more trees on fire. He fired it again, this time down on to the ground, causing an enormous explosion of fire, which consumed most of the plantation. Once again it breathed out of its mouth its destructive fiery breath, setting more mountains on fire. It moved on and on, toppling trees and structures, tearing up the countryside, and destroying everything in its way. People were running everywhere in chaos and confusion. It torched the entire countryside with its flaming breath as well as all the mountains and trees and ruined all the land that you spent years working on. Then it returned to the lake. And I alone have escaped to tell you!"

They all ran back to the castle. They got back to the farm and saw it was completely devastated. Smoke and small fires were still smoldering into the air. All of the houses and trees were lying on the ground in ruins. The land, forest, and mountains were all charred black and scorched beyond belief. Job thought to himself, *It will take years, probably decades, for this land to be able to nurture anything again.*

But this was not the worst of it. They walked across the ruined farm, toward the house of their eldest son and saw it was lying on the ground in pieces. Underneath the splintered lumber and stone, their children were all lying dead. Sitidos fell to the ground on her knees, then flat on her face, screaming and crying uncontrollably. She got up and ran into the distance, screaming and crying, then picked up a rock and was going to hit herself in the forehead with it to commit suicide. But the messengers ran out and stopped her. She continued to scream and cry while holding her head in her hands, then fainted in the messenger's arms.

Job fell to his knees, then screamed aloud, "My God! My God! Have we not always tried to do good and to be just in your eyes? How then could you ever have allowed this to happen to us? Why? Why? Why, Yahweh, are you putting us through this?" Then Job stopped crying, arose, tore his cloak, cut off his hair with a huge piece of broken glass from the ground, then threw dirt in his face and over his head. He fell to the ground and worshipped. He said, "Naked I came forth from my mother's womb and naked shall I go back there. The Lord gave and the Lord has taken away. Blessed be the name of the Lord!" In all this, Job did not sin nor did he charge God with doing wrong.

On another day, when all the angels, servants of God, and members of the divine council came to present themselves to the Lord in worship, Satan again suddenly appeared in their midst. Once again, all of paradise was filled with the sounds of the choirs of heaven singing their otherworldly hymns and chants to him. God looked out and saw that it was good and was very pleased. Then the Lord saw Satan in the midst of all the heavenly bodies.

The Lord said to Satan, "Where have you been?"

Then Satan answered the Lord, saying, "Roaming the earth and prowling amongst it, seeking the ruin of souls."

The Lord said to Satan, "Have you noticed my servant, Job? There is no one on earth like him, blameless and upright, fearing God and avoiding evil. He still holds fast to his innocence, although you incited me against him to ruin him for nothing."

But Satan answered the Lord and said, "Skin for skin! All that a man has, he will give for his life. But put forth your hand and touch his bone and his flesh. Then, surely, he will curse you to your face."

And the Lord said to Satan, "He is in your power. Only spare his life."

So Satan went forth from the presence of the Lord and all in his heavenly kingdom and returned to the presence of Job on earth. Satan struck Job with severe and painful boils on his skin from the soles of his feet to the crown of his head.

About a week later, Sitidos and Job were waking up one morning at dawn, underneath a tree in the forest. Both reeked very strongly of body odor and felt soaked and chilled to the bone from the fresh morning dew. Sitidos had since found work as a maidservant for a wealthy family. She sat up and coughed. She rose to her feet and then grumbled, "We could both sure use a bath." She leaned against a tree and began to gag and cough up clumps of thick yellow mucus. She said to Job, "How am I ever going to make it today? I feel like I'm really getting sick." She saw Job lying on his right side, facing away from her on the cold ground, shivering under a blanket. She said, "Why you, lazy! You don't care if I live or die! All you care about is your precious God who has most obviously deserted you." She went down to a nearby stream and washed her face and hands in it. She got a bucket and walked over to a well, filled it with fresh water, and took it to the family that she worked for.

Job dozed off again. Then a couple of hours later, intense itching and soreness on his skin woke him up. He kept shivering from the cold under his blanket. He sat up on the ground and began scratching very vigorously, all over his body. He said to himself, "What is going on here? This constant itching is driving me mad." He looked at his fingers, and they were all bloody from sores. He sprung to his feet and ran down to the stream and saw his reflection in the water. He screamed! He was covered from head to foot with sores boils and welts while blood and pus oozed from the sores.

Just then, Sitidos came back, looked at him and screamed. She put her hands over her mouth and nose and began coughing and gagging. She said, "It smells terrible!"

The sores were on his scalp and all over his body. He kept itching and scratching and bleeding terribly. He sat down among the scattered ashes and debris from the Leviathan's rampage and picked up a piece of broken pottery from the ground and began scraping the sores off of his body with it. And still, he did not curse God nor charge him with doing wrong. Sitidos screamed at him, saying, "You're sickening! Don't do that! Don't spread your disease to me! I don't want it! I don't want anything from you! In all my life, I never heard of a wife who has to support her husband! Get out of here! Out of my sight, now, you damn sickening creature! And just look at you! Are you still holding to your innocence? Curse God and die!"

But he said to her, "You speak as a fool would. We accept good things from God. Should we not accept evil as well?"

And through all this, Job did not sin in what he said. She lashed out at him, hitting him with her fists, and screamed, "You! You! You brought this all upon us with your God! Get out of here! Get out of my sight and never come back! Go! You disgusting wretched creature! I never want to see you again!"

As sick as he was, Job picked up his blanket and the clothes that he had left and walked away from her, across the stream, and toward the mountains as Sitidos kept screaming and cursing at him while throwing stones and sticks at his back.

He walked up over the mountains and down the other side and, finally, into the desert. He walked for a whole day and a half in the desert. He would stop occasionally and drink the water from cactus plants. He'd stagger back up on his feet to walk again, if for nothing else than to search for a shady place. On and on he tread. Once one of the wealthiest men in the world, now a nomad, a diseased sickened creature, a man cast out, a man without a family, a man without a home, a man without a country, even a man without a God. He walked on for many miles. He walked up on to the top of a burning, blistering sand dune under the sweltering hot sun, a man without hope. Finally, from hunger, his legs began to buckle under him. He could go on no more. He fell forward, face down, into the burning sand, beaten, broken, defeated, and humiliated beyond belief. The last thing he remembered before he passed out was begging God to take him.

Sometime later, he found himself waking up inside of a strange room inside of a hut. He groaned and moved in his bed. He lifted his head and saw a door leading to the outside, straight ahead of him. Then in the window of the door appeared a strange human face. He looked around the room and saw several other human faces looking in on him from outside of the room. They all kept gazing at him for several moments until he began to feel very uneasy. He noticed, outside the window in the door, a human figure pushing the face and head aside, and the door opening. A young man, dressed in modest but well-taken care of clothes, entered the room and approached him.

He extended his hand and said, "Hello, my name is Azariah."

Job turned back around and saw all the faces, still looking in the windows.

Azariah said, "Okay, all of you go on now. Back to what you were doing."

They all left. Azariah asked, "What is your name?"

"Job," he replied. Still half weary, Job asked, "Who are you? And who are all of these people looking in at me? Where am I? Where are we?"

Azariah answered, "You were found more dead than alive in the middle of the burning hot desert. We brought you here and have been tending to and feeding you for about a day and a half now. What happened to you?"

Job answered, "I lost my wife, home, and entire family due to a series of calamities that swept over my land. You see, the Chaldeans invaded my home, destroyed everything I worked for and earned, then killed my family and, finally, drove me into the desert. So who are you?"

Azariah said, "There is plenty of time for me to explain to you later just who we are. Right now, just get some sleep."

Job put his head back and went to sleep. Over the next few days, Azariah and other people nursed him back to health, giving him food and water and fresh clothing.

Three days later, Job was nearly all better, feeling fine, and his skin was almost completely cleared up from the blisters and burns he suffered. Again Azariah came in and asked how he was feeling today.

Job replied, "Much better now. Thank you. I want to say thank you to all of you who tended to me and helped me get well. Thank you all again, and God bless you all."

Azariah answered, "That's fine."

Job said, "You all did not have to do this. Thank you again for doing this for an absolute stranger. I'm forever grateful."

But Azariah, again, said, "That's okay."

After Azariah allowed Job to wash himself, he took him outside, and they walked across the campsite and into Azariah's tent. Job noticed many tents all around the grounds as people outside were working and cultivating food and building small wooden houses to live in. He could see the desert in the distance, but they were living in a forest area with trees, lakes, and running streams, much like his homeland. Azariah then explained to Job, saying, "We, as a people, don't really have a name. Many years ago, we were driven from our home, too, by the Babylonians. My parents used to tell me and my siblings that we are actual descendants of King David and Solomon. But I don't know if that is really true. Anyway, we believe in and worship Yahweh, just like you. We are a very simple people, as you can see, and everyone earns his keep here through hard work and by carrying out all the assignments he is given each day. Most of these people are not physically well. They have ailments. Some are not well in their minds. But they are all capable of working, and each fulfills his and her mission on a daily basis."

Job said, "I would be more than willing to live and work here if you will allow it and if you need the help."

Azariah replied, "I think so. We can always use the help. But remember, you will not be paid anything. You will, however, be provided food and lodging for your work. At the end of each day, you will tally your work and turn the numbers into us, and you must meet our goals. At the end of each week, we will review your numbers. And if you reach your goal, you will be fine. However, if you don't, we will talk to you and try to help you improve. After three chances, if you still are not reaching our expectations, you will be asked to leave the camp. We can't have people, especially strangers, living here for nothing or doing less work than everyone else. Does this seem fair to you?"

Job replied, "Yes."

Azariah said, "Do you think you can do it?"

Job, "I'm sure I can." Judging from the work he saw other people doing, Job was very confident he could do it.

Azariah took Job around and introduced him to everyone and said, "He will be joining our camp."

Everyone seemed to welcome him warmly and sincerely. Azariah took Job back to his tent to introduce him to his wife, Jezebel. Jezebel was inside the tent, kissing another man. She noticed Azariah coming and said to the man, "Quick, Gaddi, out the back way."

He ducked out the back door, just as Azariah showed Job into the front door first, and Job noticed the tall ruggedly handsome and muscular man exiting quickly through the back door. But Azariah never noticed anything unusual. He proceeded to show Job into the tent and introduced him to his wife and said, "He will be joining us."

Jezebel, a very beautiful but witchy and seductive-looking woman with thin piercing eyes looked straight at Job with a glare of hatred and said, "Hello. Welcome."

Azariah asked Jezebel if she was comfortable, and she replied, "As always, yes, of course. I'm just doing the usual sewing and housework."

Azariah kissed her and took Job outside. Jezebel opened the back door, then brought Gaddi back in. She said to him, "I don't know what it is, but I don't like his new man. In fact, I hate him. I have since the second I turned and laid eyes on him. I just feel he's going to be trouble."

Gaddi smiled down at Jezebel and said, "Well, if he is, we'll just have to get rid of him by making him look bad before Azariah."

The two embraced and kissed.

For the next few weeks, Job lived and worked happily and comfortably amongst these new but very easy to get along with people in his life. For the first time, in a long time, he was happy. He often even thought to himself, *This is wonderful. I could live and work here for the rest of my life.* He got down on his knees and thanked Yahweh for all these blessings. At the end of every day and week, Job tallied up his work and turned the numbers in to Azariah. He always and very easily achieved the goals set for him.

At the end of another week, he turned in his tallies to Azariah. He was not in the tent, but Jezebel was. He asked for Azariah, but Jezebel told him that he wasn't here now and to give the tallies to her. So he did and left. She looked down at the papers in her hands, and with an angry look on her face, hit her fist on the table. Gaddi came in the tent, and they embraced and kissed and began making love very passionately. Jezebel told Gaddi, "I finally figured it out. He's just so old and repulsively ugly. I can't stand the very sight of him. His ugly gray thinning hair, that white bushy unkempt beard, those sickening eyes, and that wrinkled ugly flesh still scarred from bums and blisters, all just make me sick. He just repulses me, and I hate him like I've hated no other. She put her head back and giggled and laughed long and hard, saying, "He's just so old and ugly and scrawny-looking. Isn't he a prize?" She laughed again. "How attractive!" Then she got serious and said, "Besides, he's so godly and good. I hate him. He has to go. I have a plan to get rid of him, but I'll need your help."

At the end of the next week, as Job turned in his tallies for the week, he noticed that his numbers were a bit beneath what they normally had been. He then also recalled that he was receiving less work; that is, less wood and bricks to work with than usual. He thought, *Oh well, it's just one of those things. We all have bad days, even bad weeks. I'll make it up next week.* Nonetheless, he turned in his tallies for the week.

The next week, he noticed, every day, that Gaddi was delivering to him less wood and bricks to work with. He asked him why. But Gaddi would never answer him. By the last two days of the week, he was getting only half of the load to work with than he usually was getting. As he turned in his tallies for the week, he saw that his numbers were less than half of what they used to be.

The next week, Gaddi was bringing him still less wood and bricks than usual. Again, Job put the question to him, "Why?"

But Gaddi still gave no answer. By the end of that week, Job's scores were less than half of what they used to be. Now Job felt scared and kept wondering why Gaddi was bringing him less work and why he would give him no answer to his questions and if Azariah would expel him from the colony.

The next week, Job said to himself, "I'll take matters into my own hands now." So he went and got his own work, many huge loads of brick, wood, and glass. With a smile on his face, Job began to work as usual.

But later, Gaddi came and took it all away from him and, moments later, brought him back only one small load of work. Gaddi said to Job, "You must do this! If you do not, there will be very unpleasant consequences for you."

Still, the next day, Job collected his own pile of work again, even a larger load than he had collected for himself the previous day. But, once again, Gaddi came and took it all away from him and brought him a very small pile of work that no one could possibly make his numbers with. Angrily, Job thought in his mind, *I'm going to have it out with this guy and ask him why he's doing this and demand an answer.*

After Job's demand, Gaddi hastily answered back, "Don't be angry with me about it. Jezebel called me aside and told me to do this. So if you have any qualms about it, you are going to have to take it up with her, not me. She's the boss's wife and in charge of the workers. I'm only doing what she told me to do, so again, take it up with her."

About an hour later, Azariah called Job into his tent and asked him why his numbers were dropping so quickly from when he first started. He also said to him, "Gaddi came to me a while ago and said that you were giving him all sorts of problems and trying to take over. Is this true?"

Job then answered, "I have been getting much less work than I used to get. Gaddi has even been taking my work away from me and replacing it with much smaller loads that no one could possibly make his numbers with. And while doing all of this, he's leaving everyone else alone and letting them do the work they want! It is not my fault I'm not getting the work I need to keep my numbers up! And I was not trying to take over. I was simply asking Gaddi why he was doing this!"

Azariah replied, "And what did Gaddi say?"

Job, again, answered, "He said that it was your wife, Jezebel, who told him to do this, and if I have problems with it, that I should take it up with her. Again, I don't know why she is doing this. It's like she is deliberately trying to sabotage me!"

Azariah asked, "Have you taken it up with her, Jezebel, I mean?"

Job answered, "No!" Bowing his head in humility, he went on, "I was afraid I would anger you."

Angrily, Azariah began to bawl Job out, saying, "Don't you ever speak ill or wrongly of my wife and friend! I don't believe you! You are lying to hide your own laziness! Besides, I don't care. It doesn't matter how much work you get. You have to keep up your tallies like everyone else. I told you that the first day you started with us. We are trying to build a decent community here for ourselves, and we don't want anyone here who is going to lie or be a troublemaker or not do his part! Again, I've told you all of this before!"

Job answered, "But I swear, I'm not trying to do any of these things! I'm telling you the entire truth! And I have seen for myself, your wife, Jezebel, and Gaddi kissing passionately in the tent! Again, I never told you this because I didn't want to anger you!"

Screaming at Job, and with his face turning bloodred, Azariah said, "I can't believe I trusted you at the start! I know my wife and best friend! They'd never do any of this! I ought to throw you out of here right now! But I made a promise to you to give you three chances like everyone else! So I'm not! But since you have lied so greatly, I'm only going to give you one more chance! Besides, I myself make sure at the start of every day that the work is all distributed evenly!"

Job said, "Yes, but Gaddi, at the demands of Jezebel, makes sure that I get a lot less when it is distributed to the workers!"

Hitting his fist on the table, Azariah hollered, "They do not!"

Job said, "I'm not going to give in to this, and I'm certainly not lying! My own two eyes tell me something altogether different! Now you have asked me why I'm not making my expected tallies, and I have told you! Now the rest is up to you."

Azariah answered, saying, "Now leave this tent at once! And just remember, you only have one more chance."

As Job left the tent, he heard an evil giggle coming from Jezebel's tent and Gaddi's voice, saying, "Good, it's working!"

Jezebel said, "I hate him!"

Not wishing to go through this anymore and knowing all too well that the situation would never change and that Azariah would never believe him over his wife and best friend, Job decided to leave the camp the next morning.

While gathering his belongings and some pails of water, Job saw Gaddi and Jezebel coming toward him in the dark, laughing and saying, "It worked, little man!" They seized him and dragged him out of the camp and into the desert. Gaddi punched him in the stomach and then again. While Jezebel held his arms back, Gaddi continuously struck Job in the face with his fists until the old man fell to the ground, then both simultaneously administered unto Job a life-threatening beating. They dragged him back to the camp and dropped him onto the ground again. Jezebel bitterly said to Job, "If you say anything of this to Azariah or anyone, you won't be so lucky. We'll kill you!" They left him lying on the ground and retired to their tents for the night.

The next morning at dawn, Jezebel and Gaddi ran into Azariah's tent where he worked and said, "Azariah, come fast. Job is lying on the ground. It looks like he's been hurt bad."

Surprised, Azariah rose up, and Jezebel and Gaddi took him to Job. Looking down at him, Azariah felt pity and remorse for yelling at him the night before and asked, "What could have happened to him?"

Jezebel said, "I saw him last night after dark, walking toward the desert. He may have been just going for a walk. Probably bandits seized him and then dragged him back here. There are bandits in the desert, you know. And they have been known to do these things. We better watch out for ourselves and keep vigil at night."

Azariah said, "I've never known of bandits to be around here."

Gaddi said, "That doesn't mean that there are none."

Jezebel said, "Yes, you never do know!"

They took him into a tent and placed him on a bed. After a whole day of nursing and taking care of him, they asked him what had happened. He told them the truth. Azariah, again, grew extremely angry and said to Job, "How dare you lie again! Twice I've taken you in and nursed you back to health, and this is how you repay me? By lying to me about my wife? Anyway, both Jezebel and Gaddi came to me this morning, frantic, and told me you were hurt! If they did this, why then would they tell me this? And why would they bring you back here?"

Again Job answered, saying, "Simply to make it look good."

Azariah asked Job if he was well enough to leave the tent and walk.

Job, in turn, answered, "Yes."

Azariah, firmly but politely, asked Job to leave now. They handed him his belongings and two pails of water. Job walked out of the tent through the forest, and again, back into the desert. He walked until after dark, and again, exhausted, he fell into the hot desert sand and fainted.

A few hours later, Job found himself being woken up by the desert's freezing cold night air. Shivering, he sat up then stood up. Immediately he felt a much deeper and different type of chill; one that he felt to the bone and that he felt as being pure evil. He turned around and saw human footprints being imprinted into the sand by some unseen being and coming closer and closer to him. They stopped just a few feet in front of him. Then, out of thin air, appeared a man whom he initially liked and trusted. Is it? He could barely see him in the dark, although he vaguely recognized him. Job asked, "Azariah, is that you?"

Azariah replied, "Yes, it is."

Job asked, "What are you doing way out here? And how did you find me?"

Again, Azariah replied, "I've come to tell you that you were right all along and to say I apologize and ask you to come back to camp. Now come closer, and let's renew our friendship."

Job asked, "But how could you have been making footprints in the sand if I couldn't see you?"

Azariah laughed and said, "Oh, my dear friend, Job. You're cynical about everything. That must have just been a mirage or a dream. You've been out here in the desert so long your eyes are playing tricks on you. Sure, you saw me. You just don't remember because you are so fatigued. Now, come on, let's go."

Job leaned to his left and saw a large scar on the right side of Azariah's face that he was trying to hide in the dark. Job said, "You are not Azariah! I know who you are!" Job threw sand in the man's face, turned, and quickly ran away. He then prayed, "Yahweh, I thank you for giving me the wisdom I need and for you allowing me to know right from wrong. I also thank you for distinguishing for me this mark of the true devil."

An extremely enraged Azariah dissolved into bright dust-like particles, which fell into the desert sands below. Then out of the sands emerged a large desert cobra, which expanded its neck and went slithering through the sands and up over the dunes in pursuit of Job. Finally, Job decided to retire again. He found a comfortable place, lay down, and then covered himself with a blanket. He then immediately fell asleep. As he rolled over, his left hand fell into the sand. The cobra then approached the hand and was ready to strike the back of it. But just then, God allowed the piece of parchment that Job had in his left pocket, containing the prayer to Mikhael, the archangel, to fall out, onto the sand. A bright ray of light extended from the parchment into the snake's face. The cobra was repelled immediately and crawled off in the opposite direction.

The next morning, when it was completely light out, Job felt himself being poked by a stick. He woke up and saw it was a middle-aged man, poking at him and asking if he was all right. He replied, "Yes," got up, and rubbed his eyes. He saw a carriage behind the man, which had two horses tied to the front of it. Job could not get a clear look at the man's face because the brightness of the rising sun was in his eyes. Job moved a bit to his left as the man's head blocked out the sun's rays.

The man asked again, "Are you sure you are all right?"

Again, Job answered, "Yes, I think so. But I'm very hungry and thirsty. Do you have any food and water with you?"

He answered, "Yes, come on. My name is Uriah, and yours?"

"It's Job," he answered.

Uriah asked, "Is that yours on the ground?"

Job looked down and saw it was the parchment with the prayer on it. He then answered, "Yes," bent down, picked it up, put it in his pocket, and Uriah helped him into the back of his wagon.

There were two other people in the bed of the wagon. One was a young woman in her early twenties, and the other was a teenage boy who was crippled. Uriah looked at Job and said, "Your skin is covered with blisters from the sun. How long have you been out in the desert alone?"

"A long time," Job answered.

Uriah said, "It looks it." He gave Job food and water, then laid him down on a bed and put cold rags and compresses on his skin. Job thanked him, and Uriah said, "With a few days of shade and care, you should be all right." Introducing him to the two young people, he said, "This is Kara and Timothy. Our existence is meager. And we and a few other families live in a small camp together in a forest a few miles from here. Kara and Timothy are not related, but they're very close, and Kara watches over him. She treats him like he's her kid brother. Timothy was born lame. They were the children of some of our neighbors who died in a plague some years ago. Since then, my wife and I have taken them in and raised them." Timothy, a very thin and sickly-looking child, rarely talked, but Kara came across to Job as being very spoiled and bratty. And she was because Uriah and his wife felt so sorry for her and gave her anything she wanted. Kara cast Job a dirty look of resentment from across the inside of the wagon bed as Uriah went up front and began to drive back to the camp.

When they got there, the shady trees of the forest were a welcomed sight to Job as was a spring of running water and a well with a bucket hanging over it. Uriah introduced Job to his wife, Naomi. He told Job to take it easy for a while. Job lay down, and Kara came over to him and said, "Uriah just told Naomi that there is no hope for you. You are going to die. So you better leave right now and die in the desert alone. Surely you don't want to burden them with your death. You can't be that selfish. Go now and leave them be." She put her hands over her face and then pretended to cry.

Job answered, "But he told me I was going to be all right. And I'm beginning to feel fine now."

Kara said, "He told you that just to make you feel good and not to worry you. But you are going to die, so you better leave now." She spread her fingers apart in front of her right eye and glanced down at

Job. Job motioned with his index finger for her to come closer. She did. He picked up a cup of water and threw it in her face, for he knew she was being insincere. Startled, she screamed.

Later that evening, Uriah came to Job and asked, "What can you do?"

"Almost anything," he replied. "I can chop wood, plant, cultivate, harvest, and even do carpentry and brick laying. I've done it all."

Uriah said, "You can stay and live here, if you please."

Job replied, "I'd like that, at least for a little while until I decide what I am going to do and where I'll move on to."

For the next several days, Job lived with these people and worked for them, earning his keep under the guidance of Uriah. But Kara grew more and more resentful of him because, in her mind, he was the cause of Uriah and Naomi spending less time with her and Timothy. And she just felt that he was an outsider and did not belong with them. Day after day, she insulted him and called him names like old geezer, ugly old man, and grandfather. At first, realizing she was little more than a child, Job simply ignored her. But after a while, it was beginning to bother him. She badgered him on and on about how sickly Timothy was and how he was taking all of Naomi and Uriah's time and attention away from him. She said, "Timothy has been lame since his birth. You are just a lazy old man who doesn't belong here and wants everything for free. You are a bad influence on him. How's he going to grow up watching you do these things? And you've been filling his mind with bad words."

He said, "What?"

She said, "He's been calling me names like harlot and slut. You taught him that!"

He said, "I don't believe he ever even called you anything like that. You're just making it all up."

She said, "You're just covering it up to save your own skin by saying he never said that. But you know he did and that you taught it to him." She went over to Timothy and put her arm around him and said, "I love Timothy. And you, you decrepit diseased old goat, are not going to take him away from me like you took Uriah and Naomi away from us. You stink! I hate you! And you're so ugly!" She threw an apple at him.

Job laughed in her face and said, "Go to bed, little girl. It's way past your bedtime."

She stormed away.

All day the next day, as Job worked, Kara was hiding behind trees and fences while eating fruit and throwing seeds as well as sticks and stones at him, hitting him in the head, face, back, butt, and everywhere while howling with laughter. Whenever he'd turn around and look at her, she'd give him a nasty look.

Job went and told Uriah about it, saying, "She seems to think that I took you away from her and Timothy. I never meant to do that."

Uriah answered, "I know you didn't. Besides, you didn't take Naomi and me away from anyone. She never acted nor did anything like this before. Why should she be doing it now?"

Job answered, "She just has a genuine hatred for me."

Uriah replied, "Oh, I'm sure she doesn't. Be patient with her. She's just a little jealous, that's all. And she had a very hard childhood. She was greatly traumatized by the death of her parents."

Job said, "I will not be belittled by nor argue with nor be intimidated by a child. I just wish you'd talk to her."

He said, "All right, I will. But again, I never knew her to behave like this until you came."

Job replied, "You've helped me a lot, and I greatly appreciate it. And, again, I thank you and I thank God for you and your graciousness and hospitality and for a chance to work again and to earn my keep. But please, just talk to her. It's getting to the point where I hate to get up and do my job. Please just keep her away from me!"

He said, "All right, I'll talk to her."

Later that day, Uriah called Kara in, sat her down, and asked her if all this Job said she was doing was true.

She said, "Yes."

He asked her, "Why are you doing this?"

She replied, "Because he doesn't belong here with us. He's a troublemaker. That dirty ugly old man comes in here, takes over, and Timothy and I don't see any of you and Naomi anymore."

He said, "But we still spend time with you."

She said, "But not near as much as before he came along. I wish you'd throw him out of here."

Uriah replied, "All right, that's enough! I'll not have you talk to your elders like that! You stay away from him now, and if you ever do have to be in his company, you will treat him with all the respect and courtesy that you treat anyone else with! Now is that clear?"

She said, "Yes."

He dismissed her.

Later, she approached Job, saying, "You sneaky dirty old man. Around here, you never go behind someone's back and tell lies about them to someone else. Timothy and I will get you for this! I swear it!"

As she turned to leave, he grabbed her arm and turned her back around. He asked firmly, "Just what is the matter with you? I never did anything to you or Timothy."

She said, "You are lazy and scheming, and you came here a very short time ago and took Uriah and Naomi's attention away from me and a little boy who needs all the love and attention he can get and made sure you got all of it because you probably got thrown out of somewhere for being lazy and dirty. You don't belong here!" She left.

The next day, she was eating fruit and spitting the seeds at Job and laughing and making Timothy laugh too.

Later that day, Uriah was returning to the campsite from an errand with Kara and Timothy in the back of the wagon. Kara was saying to Timothy, "And you can see his bones sticking out of his dirty hide." Her and Timothy both laughed. They rode into the camp and saw Job and others working. Job turned and looked up at the wagon as it went by. Kara looked at him and gave him a foul gesture with her hands and stuck her tongue out at him.

Kara told Timothy, "Now remember those words I told you to tell Uriah that Job told you to say—harlot, slut, and the others—whore and all the others. Remember?"

Timothy said, "Sure."

Kara got an idea. She thought to herself, *If I could just trick him and first make him believe that I'm sorry and that I'm his friend now, it could work.* She grinned. She approached Job who was working on a wagon in the camp yard and said to him, "Look, I'm sorry for all I said and did to you and for the way I acted. I've been watching you, and you're not so bad after all. Uriah talked to me about this, and I then promised him that I would stop it and try to get along with you. So can we just start again?"

Job answered, "Sure."

She saw Uriah coming to do his inspections and said quickly to Job, "Would you please go in the back of the wagon and get my basket for me?"

He said, "Sure."

As he went around the back of the wagon, and as Uriah came closer, Kara started to repair a broken wheel on the wagon. She said to Uriah, "I have it all fixed now, and Job said he is supposed to paint it."

Uriah said, "Yes, but I thought it was Job's assignment to fix it too."

Kara said, "That's all right. I don't mind."

That evening, as Uriah came to do the day's final inspections, Job had just finished painting the wagon. Kara came and told Job that Uriah wanted to see him about something, but she didn't know what. As he left to go see him, Uriah came and saw Kara holding the paint can and brush. She said, "It's very nice, isn't it?"

Uriah asked, "You mean you did all this?"

"Yes," she replied.

He asked, "Well, where's Job?"

She said, "I don't know. He left several hours ago, and I haven't seen him since. And I knew that you wanted this done as soon as possible, so I took it on myself to do it. Was that all right?"

Uriah said, "Yes, and the next time you see Job, please tell him I want to talk to him."

She said, "I will."

Uriah walked away while Kara stood there, giggling to herself.

The next morning, Job was told to cut a field of sugarcane. The man in charge handed him the machete, and he went to work. It took him several hours, most of the morning. When he was finished, he was exhausted and sat down for a moment on a rock and was wiping the sweat off of his face and brow. Then Kara whispered to Timothy, "All right, now quick, before Uriah comes, go down on your crutches and take a machete and stand in front of the field and act like you just cut it."

So he did. As he was standing with the machete in his hand, Uriah asked him, "Timothy, did you do all this by yourself?"

He said, "No, Kara and I both did it."

Uriah saw Job dozing off and said, "Good job, Timothy."

Kara said out loud, "How hard little Timothy worked while that big clumsy lazy lummox, Job, just slept."

Job heard it and became wide awake. He said firmly to Uriah, "I'd like to see you in private for a moment."

Kara rushed over and said, "No, no, Uriah, I must see you first, and then Job can!"

Uriah said, "Very well. Let's go."

Job was waiting outside of Uriah's cabin for a long while, then he finally knocked on the door. Uriah opened the door. Job stepped in and saw Kara sitting at a table, crying and sobbing very intensely. Naomi was rubbing her head and back, trying to comfort her. Uriah looked at Job and said, "I think you better leave now. Please just go."

He replied, "But why?"

Uriah shouted at Job, saying, "Kara told us that you made sexual advances to her! And that you've been doing it since you came here, and that several times, you even tried to touch her!"

Job shouted back, "I most certainly never did!"

Uriah said, "And I've even found you sleeping on duty and not at your post and getting other people, these two young children, to do your work! That's not why you are here, you know! And Timothy has been using all kinds of foul language, bad words that he never even dreamed of saying! And when we asked him where he got them from, he said you told him to say them! He never could have picked up language like that from anyone here but you! He never said these things until you came!"

Naomi said, "And you haven't been coming to see us when we told Kara to tell you to come, and you came when we didn't ask for you! What kind of sick crazy man are you? So, again, please just go!"

Job replied, "All right, I will right now, but none of this is true! I would never corrupt a youngster's mind like that, and no one ever told me to come and see you! Kara never told me any of this! She's the one who's been doing this and scheming behind our backs, trying to make me look bad in front of you, and poisoning this young boy's mind!"

Uriah shouted back, "How dare you take advantage of two young children and blame your wrongdoing on them!"

Job said, "It was not my wrongdoing, it was Kara's!"

Uriah punched Job straight in the mouth. As Job thrust back at him, Uriah struck him hard with the back of his hand, knocking him over, backward to the floor, turning over a table and chair, and rendering him unconscious.

The next thing Job remembered was waking up in the back of a wagon to a very bumpy ride. The wagon stopped. Uriah opened the back curtain, grabbed Job by the back of his neck and belt, picked him up, pulled him out of the wagon, and threw him face down onto the hot sand.

Uriah said, "I'm throwing you back out into the desert where you came from and where trash like you belongs!"

Job got up, brushed himself off, and said, "Please just listen to me!"

Again, Uriah struck him in the face with the back of his hand, and Job fell backward and rolled down over a sand dune. He heard the wagon riding away. Again, he got up, brushed himself off, and climbed back up the sand dune. He saw the back of the wagon in a distance, getting farther away, and Kara and Timothy sitting in it, grinning and laughing at him. Job walked back down the sand dune, picked up his basket, put it over his right shoulder, and sat down in the sand, feeling traumatized, humiliated, and frustrated beyond belief, and totally bewildered. As he sat there, he heard the voice of the Lord, saying, "Job, return to your home at once and as soon as you can. Your suffering is nearly over." So he got up and once again began crossing the vast desert alone and on foot.

After several hours of walking in the baking hot sun, Job sat down and rested a while. Then he heard footsteps behind him. He turned around and looked and saw another stranger walking down a sand dune toward him. He got up, looked at the man's face, and saw no scar there. Job felt relieved and happy that this man was not Satan and that the Lord told him to go home and that his suffering was nearly over. The man introduced himself as Aben, and Job told him his name. He asked Job, "Think you could use some company?"

Job replied, "Certainly!"

So they walked on together. During their journey, Job told him everything that had happened to him. Then he asked, "How about you?"

Aben answered, "I'm just a simple wanderer, a drifter, going from place to place, never staying in one area for very long. I like to live this way. There is no one to answer to. I can do what I want to, when I want to. There is not much for me to tell you about myself. Only that I was born in Palestine. Actually, I'm going back there. I'd like to see the place one last time before I die and maybe even make that my final place of residence."

Job asked, "Are you going to die?"

Aben laughed and said, "Not yet, I hope. But I'm tired now of wandering, and I'm familiar with Palestine, and I know people there. So maybe I can do something useful and that I enjoy there for a living."

Job said, "I certainly have not been able to find anything like that yet."

Again, Aben laughed and asked, "So you were thrown out of two places, ha? Well, you're probably better off on your own without any of those people."

Job excitedly said, "Palestine is on this side of Uz where my home is and where I'm returning to. Can we walk together that far?"

"Yes, that's fine with me," Aben replied. On their way, Aben was continuously talking to Job about self-respect and trying to restore his faith and confidence in himself. He also said, "God allowed all this to happen to you for a very good reason, and that you may not understand now, but you will someday.

Aben's words made Job feel good and did, indeed, restore his faith in God and in himself. Job thought to himself, *This man must be an angel of God sent to me.* He said, "Thank you, God! Thank you, God, for this man as a companion."

After dark, they settled down in an open place, lay down and talked for a while, then went to sleep.

A few hours later after dark, a scorpion came crawling through the sand toward Job and Aben while they slept on the ground. It approached the back of Job's knee, raised its tail, and was ready to sting his bare leg. Job, sleeping on his right side, rolled over, and again, the piece of parchment with the prayer on it rolled out of the left pocket in his robe and fell onto the ground. Again, a ray of bright light shot out from the rolled-up parchment and directly struck the peering scorpion head-on. This repelled it away from Job, and it turned and approached Aben. He, too, was sleeping on his right side, turned over, and his left leg partially sunk into the sand right in front of the scorpion. The venomous killer at once raised its tail and stung Aben, just below the left knee.

Aben shouted in pain, immediately woke up, and screamed out loud while holding his left leg. Job woke up, heard him screaming, and ran over to him. Aben continued holding his leg, screaming in pain and horror, shouting, "Help me, Job! My God, help me! Help me! Something bit me!"

Job saw the scorpion on the ground and, right away, ran over and killed it by repeatedly crushing it with his foot and stomping it into the ground by the heel of his boot. Aben kept screaming as violent convulsions erupted all through his body. As his body kept trembling more violently, white foam and saliva sprouted forth from his mouth. Over and over, he screamed, "Job, help me! Make it stop! Make it stop!"

Job straightened out his left leg and saw in the moonlight, right below his left knee, what looked like a huge black burnt lump. Job tore a long thin piece of his clothing off and wrapped it around

Aben's leg, right above the knee, and pulled as hard as he could on both ends of it, squeezing his leg in order to cut off the flow of blood to his heart. Job saw the upper part of his leg turning purple. He pulled harder. But Aben's violent tremors only got worse, and his screams were even hurting Job's eardrums.

Finally, the convulsions stopped, and Aben became calm and died. Job noticed more white saliva all over his face as he lay there, dead. Job raised his head and screamed as loud as he could into the air, "Why? Why? Why? Why, God, this good decent and innocent man? Why? For what reason?" He clenched both fists, screamed again into the air and, in a fit of anger and rage, began kicking and throwing sand in all different directions. Then he laid his head on Aben's chest and wept bitterly.

The next morning, after sunrise, Job dug a huge deep hole in the sand, rolled Aben's body into it, then covered it back up. He calmly knelt beside the grave and said a few prayers. He glanced to his left and saw the pieces of the crushed scorpion on the ground. He could very plainly see the tail and two pincers.

Then right before his eyes, in the same spot, were two human legs. He stood up, and to his shock, overwhelming joy, and astonishment, he saw directly in front of him his eldest and most beloved and trusted son, Daniel. And beside him stood his first and most favored daughter, Elizabeth. Job began to weep, and tears streamed down his face, and he spoke, "But how? How can this be? You are both here right before me and very much alive! How can this be? You were both killed! How, how is your mother?"

Daniel replied, "She is well. We are taking good care of her."

Job answered, "Thank God."

They both said, "Father, we've come to take you home to her. She is waiting for you."

Job felt nothing now but joy and relief. Then, suddenly, a strong gust of wind shot by and blew their long hair away from their faces. Job instantly saw a long deep scar on both of their faces. But at the sheer joy of seeing his two most beloved children, his entire mind and body felt like they were just melting into total vulnerability. He thought to himself, *I don't care if you show scars on your faces. I will never do harm to the two people I've loved most of all in this world.* He even reached his hands out to them. Then he thought, *But they both have the scars. What should I do?*

Then, just as he remembered God's promise to him about seeing a scar on the face of Satan, Daniel lowered his head slightly and gave an evil grin. Elizabeth extended her arms as Job could plainly see the scar on her face too. And she said, "Come, Father, come."

He stepped back several steps and prayed to the Lord, "God, I don't care if they kill me now. Maybe it's my time to die. As I said before, the only blessing now would be death. And I trust my soul will be taken unto your bosom. Not because of anything good that I've done or said but because of your great mercy and forgiveness." He stepped backward again, closed his eyes, and spoke, "Oh Lord, reveal the truth to me! I now believe these are not my children. May your will be done!" He opened his eyes and saw the body of Elizabeth fading away into a puff of smoke and Daniel's body being raised off of the ground and drawn backward by a powerful gust of wind until it disappeared into the horizon. "I thank you, God! Thank you, God!" Job prayed. Then he turned and continued on his trek through the desert.

He walked and rested off and on for twenty-four hours. The next afternoon, due to exhaustion and dehydration, once again, he collapsed under the boiling hot sun. He started to heave from dehydration, and his nausea became totally unbearable. He was now crawling on his belly and couldn't go on anymore. He looked up and saw an oasis directly ahead of him. He managed to push himself up by his arms and reach his right hand out to it and kept pushing his body toward it as it kept getting closer and closer. But then the word *mirage* entered his mind. *Yes,* he thought, *it has to only be a mirage that people in the desert see so often.* Again, he put his face down into the burning sand and fainted.

That evening just before sunset, he woke up. He didn't know how long he had been unconscious, but he felt more blisters on his face and chest from the hot sand, and his back felt like it was on fire. He felt like he was in a better state of mind and had his full wits this time. Again, he looked ahead and saw the oasis just like he had seen it before. He thought, *What if it is real?* He stood up and staggered over toward it and put his hand in it. It was real! Ecstatically, he screamed, "It's real! It's real! It's real! By God above, it is real! Thank you! Thank you! Thank you, God! Thank you, God, eternally because you are indeed eternal!"

He put his face in it to cool his burns. He kept throwing several handfuls of water in his face to cool and wash it. He ripped his turban off and dunked his entire head in it and washed and scrubbed it as hard as he could. He got up, dried his face and head with his turban, and drank from the cool and clear spring that fed the pool of water. He kept gulping and swallowing one mouthful of water after another as fast as he could until he nearly choked. With his thirst finally quenched, he walked over to a small forest of trees with fruit growing on them, mainly figs and berries. Again, he tore them off as fast as he could and chewed and gulped up several handfuls of them while spitting out the seeds until his belly was full. He drank more water from the spring and put his turban back on and lay down under a shady tree and went to sleep.

The next morning, he woke up and saw a hearth cake and a tall jar of water sitting on the ground. He ate up all the cake and finished all the water in the jar. He knew the Lord put the food and water there for him, overnight, otherwise the rest of his journey would be too long for him. Again, he washed and refreshed himself in the pool of cool water and knelt down and thanked God from his heart for all the blessings he had just received. After this, he filled the jar with water and his basket with fruit, and though he hated to leave the place, he moved on his way because he knew it was God's will, and that he would never let him die in the desert like this, and that his journey was mostly behind him now. As he continued on his way, he looked back and, to his astonishment, saw no oasis. There was nothing there, except burning hot sand.

After walking for several hours, he drank up all the water and ate up most of the fruit. Again, weakness began to overtake his body, and he began to feel faint. He kept saying over and over to himself, "My God, my God, I know you are not going to let me die out here in the desert alone after telling me to return home! This last part of my journey is a lot longer than I thought it would be. But still, why are you putting me through all of this?" After all of this, he could see, way ahead of him, three human forms, all walking straight toward him in the glowing white heat waves of midday. He thought again that it was a mirage. But as weak as he was, he pushed himself on to see whether it was a mirage or real. As he walked closer toward them, and they walked closer toward him, he not only came to the realization that they were real people, but he vaguely recognized them from afar.

As he got even closer, he recognized them as three childhood friends he used to have. He remembered, in a flash, the four of them all laughing while running and playing on the shady meadows of their home village. He came within a few feet of them and stopped. He recognized them instantly and could see clearly that not one of them had a scar on his face. They were indeed his old childhood friends, and he was once again overcome with joy and gladness. Job clasped their hands and hugged them. But they did not recognize him. Then they said to him, "We are Eliphaz from Teman, Bildad from Shuh, and Zophar from Naamath. We are three childhood friends of Job and have heard of all the misfortune that has come upon him and have set out each one from his own place. We met and have journeyed together to find him and to give him sympathy and comfort."

Job said, "That's me! And I surely know who you all are. I'm your old childhood friend, Job! Have you come all this way just to see me?"

"Yes," they replied. Then they began to weep aloud; they tore their cloaks and threw dirt into the air over their heads. Then they found another shady meadow and sat down upon the ground with him under the trees for seven days and seven nights, but none of them in all that time spoke a word to him, for they saw how great was his suffering.

During this time, the Sabeans were camping outside in the mountains, about twenty-five or thirty miles northeast of the castle. Sitting there quietly, roasting and eating meat over their fires, they began to change their minds. One hyper rabble-rouser in the group stood up and hollered, "Why? Why did we give in to the Chaldeans and run away from them?"

Another of their group replied, "Because we were smart, not stupid. Because there were a lot more of them than us, that's why."

But he persisted, "I tell you, it's not fair. We were there first, weren't we?" Throwing his fists in the air, he continued, hollering, "I say it's not right! I say we fight! I say we return to Arabia and gather an army, as many as we need and can find, then go back to the castle and challenge those blood-sucking thieves in a battle, slay them all, and reclaim what we had before them! Right?"

Others in the group began to cheer him and holler, "Yes! Yes! We'll take back what is ours!"

He shouted, "Who are they to come and take away what is ours and to try to conquer us? If we have as many troops as they have, we will be just as strong and, maybe, even more than a match for them! So let's do it!"

They all shouted back in his favor, and the shouting rose to a heavy clamor. So they all jumped on their horses and galloped all the way back to southern Arabia and gathered as many troops as they could find.

Back at the meadow, seven days and nights had passed since Job had been reunited with his old friends. After this time, he opened his mouth and cursed his day. He spoke out and said, "Perish the day on which I was born, the night when they said, 'The child is a boy!' May that day be darkness. May God above not care for it. May light not shine upon it! May darkness and gloom claim it, clouds settle upon it, blackness of day devour it! May obscurity seize that night. May it not be counted among the days of the year nor enter into the number of the months! May that night be barren. Let no joyful outcry greet it! Let them curse it who curse the sea, those skilled at disturbing Leviathan! May the stars of its twilight be darkened. May it look for daylight but have none nor gaze on the eyes of the dawn because it did not keep shut the doors of the womb to shield my eyes from trouble! Why did I not die at birth? Come forth from the womb and expire? Had I slept, I should then have been at rest. Or why was I not buried away like a stillborn child? Like babies that have never seen the light? Only there do the wicked cease from troubling. There the weary can find rest."

Then Eliphaz the Temanite answered and said, "If someone attempts a word with you, would you mind? How can anyone refrain from speaking? Look, you have instructed many and made firm their feeble hands. Your words have upheld the stumbler. You have strengthened faltering knees. But now that it comes to you, you are impatient. When it touches you, you are dismayed. Is not your piety a source of confidence and your integrity of life your hope? Reflect now, what innocent person perishes? Where are the upright destroyed? As I see it, those who plow mischief and sow trouble will reap them. By the breath of God, they perish. And by the blast of his wrath, they are consumed.

"Though the lion roars, though the king of beasts cries out, the teeth of its young are broken. The old lion perishes for lack of prey, and the cubs of the lioness are scattered. Can anyone be more in the right than God? Can mortals be more blameless than their Maker? Look, he puts no trust in his servants, and even with his messengers, he finds fault. Human beings beget mischief as sparks fly upward. In your place, I would appeal to God, and to God I would state my plea. He does things great and unsearchable, things marvelous and innumerable. He gives rain upon the earth and sends water upon the fields. He sets up the lowly on high, and those who mourn are raised to safety. He frustrates the plans of the cunning so that their hands achieve no success. He catches the wise in their own ruses, and the designs of the crafty are routed. They meet with darkness in the daytime. At noonday, they grope as if it were night.

"But he saves the poor from the sword of their mouth, from the hand of the mighty. Thus the needy have hope, and iniquity closes its mouth. Happy the one whom God reproves! The Almighty's discipline do not reject. For he wounds, but he binds up. He strikes, but his hand gives healing. Out of six troubles, he will deliver you, and at the seventh, no evil shall touch you. In famine, he will deliver you from death. And in war, from the power of the sword. From the scourge of the tongue, you shall be hidden, and you shall not fear approaching ruin. For at ruin and want, you shall laugh. The beasts of the earth, you will fear not."

Then Job answered and said, "Ah, could my anguish be measured and my calamity laid within the scales? They would now outweigh the sands of the sea! Because of this, I speak without restraint. For the arrows of the Almighty are in me, and my spirit drinks in their poison. The terrors of God are arrayed against me. Have I no helper and has my good sense deserted me? A friend owes kindness to one in despair though he has forsaken the fear of the Almighty. My companions are as undependable as a wadi, like the watercourses that run dry in midday. Have I not cried out, 'Deliver me from the hand of the enemy, redeem me from oppressors?' Teach me, and I will be silent. Make me now understand how I have erred. How painful honest words are, yet how unconvincing is your argument! Do you still consider your words as proof? But the sayings of a weary desperate man as wind? Come now, give me your attention. Surely I will not lie to your face. Think it over, is this justice? Think it over, I still am right. Is there insincerity on my tongue?"

Job continued on, "Is not life on earth a drudgery? Its days like those of a hireling? Or is it not like a slave who longs for the shade? Or a hireling who waits for his wages? So I have been assigned months of futility and troubling nights have been counted off for me. I lie down and say, 'When shall I arise?' Then the night drags on. I am filled with restlessness until the dawn. My flesh is clothed with worms and scabs, my skin cracks and festers. My days are swifter than a weaver's shuttle. They come to an end without hope and fly away without a glimpse of joy. Remember that my life is like the wind, my eyes will not ever see happiness again. As a cloud dissolves and vanishes, so whoever goes down to Sheol shall not come up.

"Am I the sea? Or the Leviathan that he places a constant watch over me? When I say, 'My bed shall comfort me, my couch shall ease my complaint,' then you frighten me with dreams and terrify me with visions so that I shall prefer strangulation and death rather than my existence. I waste away. I will not live forever. Let me alone, for my days are but a breath. If I sin, what do I do to you, o watcher of mortals? Why have you made me your target? Why should I be burdened for you? Why do you not pardon my offense or take away my guilt? For soon I shall lie down in the dust, and should you seek me, I shall be gone."

Bildad the Shuhite answered and said, "How long shall you utter such things? The words from your mouth are a mighty wind! Does God pervert judgment? Or does the Almighty pervert justice? If your children have sinned against him, and he has not yet forgiven them, and you yourself who are blameless have recourse to God and make supplication to the Almighty, surely he will rouse himself for you and restore your rightful home. Behold, God will not cast away the upright, neither will he take the hand of the wicked. Once more will he fill your mouth with much laughter and your lips with rejoicing. Those who hate you shall be clothed with shame, and the tent of the wicked shall be no more."

Then Job answered and said, "I know well it is so. But how can anyone be in the right before God? Should one wish to contend with him, he could not answer him once in a thousand times. God is wise in heart and mighty in power. Who has withstood him and remained whole? He removes the mountains before they know it. He overturns them in his anger. He shakes the earth out of its place, and the pillars beneath it tremble. He commands the sun, and it does not rise. He seals up the stars. He made the Bear and Orion, the Pleiades and the constellations of the south. He does all things great and unsearchable, things marvelous and innumerable. Should he come near me, I do not see him. If he seizes me forcibly, who can resist? Who can say to him, 'What are you doing?' He is God, and he does not relent. The helpers of Rahab bow beneath him. How then could I give him an answer or choose out arguments against him? Even though I were right, I could not answer but should rather beg for what was due me. If I appealed to him, and he answered me, I could not believe that he would listen to me.

"With a storm, he might overwhelm me and multiply my wounds for nothing. He would not allow me to draw breath but might fill me with bitter griefs. When the scourge slays suddenly, he scoffs at the despair of the innocent. The earth is given into the hands of the wicked. He covers the faces of its judges. My days are no slower than a runner. They flee away. They see no joy or happiness. They shoot by like skiffs of reed, like an eagle swooping upon its prey. If I say I will now forget my complaining, I will lay aside my sadness and be of good cheer, then I am in dread of all of my pains, and I know that he will not hold me innocent. It is I who will be accounted guilty, so then why should I strive in vain? If I wash myself with soap and clean my hands with lye, he would plunge me in a ditch so that my garments would abhor me. And since I know that his terrors will always frighten me, and that I could never speak without being afraid of him, I loathe my life."

Job continued, "I will give myself up to complaint. I will speak from the bitterness of my soul. I will say to God: 'Do not put me in the wrong! Let me know why you oppose me. Is it a pleasure for you to oppress? To spurn the work of your hands? And shine on the plan of the wicked? Have you eyes of flesh? Do you see as mortals see? And are your years like a human lifetime that you seek for guilt in me and search after my sins even though you know that I am not wicked and that none can deliver me out of your hand? Your hands have formed and fashioned me. Will you then turn and destroy me? Oh, remember, you fashioned me from clay! Will you then turn and bring me down to dust again?

"'If I should sin, you would keep a watch on me, and from my guilt, you would not absolve me. If I'd be wicked, I'd dare not hold up my head, for I should be drenched in shame and affliction! Should I lift my head, you hunt me like a lion. Repeatedly you show your wondrous powers against me. You renew your attack upon me and multiply your endless harassment of me. In waves your troops come against me. Why then did you bring me forth from the womb? I should have died, and no eye should have seen me. I should be as though I had never lived. I should have been taken from the womb to the grave. Are not my days few? I cannot even say, "Let me alone that I may recover a little" when a horde of evildoers surround me like a pack of wolves, thirsting for human blood!'"

And Zophar the Naamathite answered and said, "Shall your babbling keep others silent and shall you deride, and no one give rebuke? But oh, that God would speak and open his lips against you and tell you the secrets of wisdom, for good sense has two sides so that you might learn that God overlooks some of your sinfulness. Can you find out the depths of God? Or can you ever find out the perfection of the Almighty?

"For he knows the worthless and sees iniquity. If you set your heart aright and stretch out your hand toward him, if iniquity is in your hands, remove it, and do not let injustice dwell in your tent. Surely then you may lift up your head in innocence, and you may stand firm and unafraid. For then you shall forget your misery, like water that has ebbed away you shall regard it. Then your life shall be brighter than the noonday. Its gloom shall become like the morning, and you shall be secure because there is hope. Then you shall lie down in safety, and no one will disturb you. Many shall entreat your favor. But the wicked, looking on, shall be consumed with envy, and escape shall be cut off from them."

Then Job answered and said, "No doubt you are people with whom wisdom shall die! But I have intelligence as well as you. I do not fall short of you, for who does not know such things as you've said? I've become the sport of my neighbors. The just, the perfect man is a laughingstock. I am disgraced before all men. Yet the tents of the robbers are prosperous, and those who provoke God are secure, whom God has in his power. With him are wisdom and might. If he knocks a thing down, it is not rebuilt. If he holds back the waters, there is a drought. If he sends them forth again, they overwhelm the land. With him there is strength and prudence. The misled and the seducers are his. He sends the counselors away barefoot and makes fools of judges. The righteous he makes wander in a pathless desert. They grope in the darkness without light. He makes them wander like drunkards."

Job continued on, saying, "All this my eye has seen, my ear has heard and perceived it. What you know, I also know. I do not fall short of you. But I would surely speak with the Almighty. I want to argue with God. But you gloss over falsehoods, you are worthless physicians, every one of you! Oh, that you would be together silent. That for you would be wisdom! Hear my argument and listen to the accusations from my lips. Is it for God that you speak falsehood? Is it for him that you utter deceit? Will it be well when he shall search you out? Can you deceive him as you do a mere human being? He will openly rebuke you and, surely, his majesty will frighten you and dread of him shall fall upon you, if in secret you show partiality!

"So be silent! Let me alone that I may speak, no matter what happens to me. I will take my life in my own hands. Slay me though he might, I will wait for him. I will defend my conduct before him. Behold I have prepared my case. I know that I am right. If anyone can make a case against me, then I shall be silent and expire. But first, there are two things I ask of you: Withdraw your hand far from me so your terror will not frighten me and, second, is only to call me, and I will respond.

"My case is this: What are my faults and my sins? My misdeeds and my sins, make known to me. Why do you hide your face and consider me your enemy? Will you harass a wind-driven leaf or pursue a withered straw? For you draw up bitter indictments against me and punish me for the faults of my youth.

"A man who is born of woman is short-lived and full of trouble, like a flower that springs up and quickly fades, swift as a shadow that does not abide. Upon such a one you set your eyes, bringing me into judgment before you? Since my days are determined, you know the number of my months. You have fixed the limit which I cannot pass. So, therefore, I plead: Look away from me and let me be, while like a hireling, I complete my day. For a tree, there is hope. If it is cut down, it will sprout again, and its tender shoots will not cease. And at the first whiff of water, it sprouts and puts forth branches again like a young plant. But when a man dies, all vigor leaves him. When a mortal expires, where then is he? As when the waters of a lake fail or a stream dries up, so mortals lie down, never to rise again. Until the heavens are no more, they shall not awake nor be roused out of their sleep.

"Oh, that you would hide me in Sheol, shelter me until your wrath has past and fix a time to remember me. If you would only call, I would answer you. Surely then, you would count my steps and not keep watch for sin in me. My misdeeds would be sealed up in a pouch, and you would cover over my guilt. As water wears away stone, and the torrents wash away the soil of the land, so you destroy the hope in mortals!"

Then Eliphaz the Temanite answered and said, "Does a wise man answer with windy opinions, or puff himself up with the east wind? Does he argue in speech that does not avail, and in words that are to no profit? You, in fact, do away with piety. You lessen devotion toward God because your wickedness instructs your mouth, and you choose to speak like the crafty. Your own mouth condemns you, not I. Your own lips refute you. Do you listen in on God's council and restrict wisdom to yourself? What do you know that we do not? Or understand that we do not? Are the consolations of God not enough for you? Why does your heart carry you away? And why do your eyes flash so that you turn your anger against God and let such words escape your mouth? How can any mortal be blameless? Or anyone born of woman be righteous? If you listen to me, I will tell you what I have seen and what the wise relate and have not contradicted since the days of their ancestors.

"The wicked is in torment all his days, and limited years are in store for the ruthless. His ears are filled with the sounds of terrors, and when all seems prosperous for him, a spoiler comes upon him. A day of darkness fills him with dread. Distress and anguish overpower him like a king expecting an attack because he has stretched out his hand against God and has so arrogantly challenged the Almighty. He shall wither before his time, his branches no longer green. He shall be like a vine that sheds its grapes unripened or like an olive tree casting off its blossoms. The breed of the impious shall be sterile, and fire shall consume the tents of all the extortioners. They conceive malice, bring forth deceit, and give birth to fraud."

Then Job answered and said, "I have heard this sort of thing many times. Troublesome comforters, all of you! Is there no end to windy words? What sickness makes you rattle on? I also could talk as you do were you in my place. I could declaim over you or wag my head at you. I could strengthen you with talk, with mere chatter, give relief. If I speak, my pain is not relieved. If I stop talking, nothing changes. My enemies throw daggers at me. They gape at me with their mouths. They strike me on the cheek with insults and are all enlisted against me. God has given me over to the impious; into the hands of the wicked he has cast me. I was in peace, but he dislodged me, seized me by the neck, and dashed me to pieces. He has set me up for a target, and his arrows strike me from all directions. He allows my enemy to pierce my sides without mercy and to pour out my gall upon the ground. He pierces me, thrust upon thrust, rushes at me like a warrior. I have sewn sackcloth on my skin, laid my horn low in the dust. My face is inflamed with weeping, darkness covers my eyes, although my hands are free from violence, and my prayer sincere. Oh that justice may be done for a mortal of God. My years are numbered, and I go the road of no return.

"My spirit is broken, my days finished, my burial at hand. Surely mockers surround me. At their provocation, my eyes grow dim. I ask you to put up a pledge for me, but no one is there to give surety for me. I am made a byword of the people. I am one at whom people spit. My eyes are blind with anguish, and my whole frame is like a shadow. I do not find a wise man among you! My days pass by, my plans are at an end with the yearning of my heart."

Then Bildad the Shuhite answered and said, "When will you put an end to words? Reflect now, and we can have a discussion. Why are we accounted like beasts, equal to them in your sight? Truly the light of the wicked is extinguished, the flame of his fire casts no light. In his tent light is darkness, the lamp above him goes out. His many vigorous steps are hemmed in, and his own counsel casts him out. His strength is famished, disaster is ready at his side, his skin is eaten to the limbs, disease and death eat his limbs. He is plucked from the security of his tent, and then marched off to the king of terrors. Fire lodges in his tent. Over his abode, brimstone is scattered.

"Below, his roots dry up and, above, his branches wither. His memory then perishes from the earth, and he has no name in the vast countryside. He is driven from light into darkness and banished from the world. He has neither offshoot nor offspring among his people, no survivor where once he dwelt. Those who come after shall be appalled at his fate. Those who went before are seized with horror. So is it then with the dwelling of the impious. Such is the place of the one who does not know God!"

Then Job answered and said, "How long will you afflict my spirit, grind me down with words? All these ten times you have humiliated me, have assailed me without shame! Even if it were true that I am at fault, my fault would remain with me. If truly you exalt yourselves at my own expense and use my shame as an argument against me, know then that it is God who has dealt unfairly with me and compassed me round with his net. If I cry out loud—violence! I am not answered. I shout for help, but there is no justice, and no one there to strengthen me nor to share in my cause. He has barred my way, and I cannot pass. He has veiled my path in darkness. He has stripped me of my glory and taken the diadem from my brow. He breaks me down on every side, and I am gone. He has uprooted my hope like a tree. He has kindled his wrath against me. He counts me one of his enemies. His troops advance as one. They build up their road to attack me and encamp around my tent. My family has withdrawn from me, my friends are wholly estranged. My relatives and companions neglect me, my guests have forgotten me.

"Even my maidservants consider me a stranger—I am a foreigner in their sight. I call my servant, but he gives no answer, though I plead aloud to him. My breath is abhorrent to my wife. I am loathsome to my very children. Even young children despise me. When I appear, they speak against me. All my intimate friends hold me in horror. Those whom I loved have now turned against me! My bones cling to my skin, and I have escaped by the skin of my teeth. Help me, help me, you, my friends, for the hand of God has struck me! Why do you pursue me like God and prey insatiably upon me? Oh would that my words be written down, inscribed in a record or chiseled in stone. As for me, I know that my vindicator lives and that he will at last stand forth upon the dust. This will happen when my skin has been stripped off and, from my flesh, I will see God! I will see for myself with my own eyes. I will behold him! My inmost being is consumed with longing."

Then Zophar the Naamathite answered and said, "So now my thoughts provide an answer for me because of the deep feelings within me. Do you not know this from of old, since human beings were placed upon the earth, the great triumph of the wicked is short and the joy of the impious is only but for a moment? Though his pride mounts up to the heavens and his head reaches to the clouds, he perishes forever like the dung he uses for fuel, and onlookers say, 'Where is he?' Like a demon, he takes flight and cannot be found. He fades away like a vision of the night. Though wickedness is sweet in his mouth, and he hides it under his tongue and retains it and will not let it go, in his stomach, his food shall turn, and it will become like venom of asps inside him. The riches he swallowed, he shall vomit up, for God shall make his belly disgorge them. The poison of asps he shall drink in, and the viper's fangs shall slay him. He shall see no streams of oil, no torrents of honey or milk. He shall give back his gains, never used, like his profit from trade, never enjoyed.

"Because he has oppressed and neglected the poor and has stolen a house he has not built and has known no quiet in his greed, he shall never be able to save himself in his treasure. Therefore his prosperity shall not endure. When he has more than enough, distress shall be his, and every sort of trouble shall befall him. When he has filled his belly, God shall send against him every sort of wrath and rain down his missiles upon him. Should he escape an iron weapon, a bronze bow shall pierce him. All sorts of terrors shall fall upon him, and complete darkness will be in store for his treasured ones. A fire not fanned shall consume him, and any survivor in his tent shall be destroyed. The heavens shall reveal his guilt, and the earth rise up against him. All of this is the portion of the wicked, the heritage appointed him by God."

Then Job answered and said, "If a man were to die and live again to bring me comfort and restoration, all the days of my drudgery, I would wait for my relief to come. At least listen to my words and bear with me while I speak then. After that, you can mock me! Is my complaint toward any human being? Why should I not be impatient? Look at me and be appalled. I am dismayed and shuddering seizes my flesh. Why do the wicked keep on living, grow old, and become mighty in power? Their progeny is secure in their sight, their offspring are before their eyes. Their homes are safe without fear, and the rod of God is not upon them. Their bulls breed without fail. Their cows calve and never do they miscarry. Their young run free like sheep and do not trip. They sing and make merry to the sound of the pipe. They live out their days in prosperity and tranquilly go down to Sheol.

"Yet they say to God, 'Depart from us, for we have no desire to know your ways! What is the Almighty that we should serve him?' Their happiness is not in their own hands. The designs of the wicked are far from me! How often is their fire quenched? And how often does destruction befall them? But I say: 'Let their own eyes behold their calamity, and the wrath of the Almighty, let them drink in!' Yet on the day of calamity and the wrath of the Almighty, the evil man is spared. How empty the consolation you offer me! Your arguments remain a fraud."

Then again, Eliphaz the Temanite answered and said, "Can a man, especially a wise man, be profitable to God? Does it please the Almighty that you are just? Does he gain if your ways are perfect? Is it because of your piety that he reproves you? That he enters into judgment with you? Is not your wickedness great, your iniquity endless? You keep your relatives' goods in pledge unjustly, leave them stripped naked of their clothing. When was the last time you gave a drink of cold water to the thirsty? And from the hungry you withhold bread, as if the land had belonged to the powerful, and only the privileged could dwell in it! You sent widows away empty-handed and destroyed the resources of the orphans. Therefore snares are all around you, sudden terror makes you panic, and a deluge of water covers you! Does not God, in the heights of the heavens, behold the top of the stars, high though they are? Yet you say, 'What does God know? Thick clouds hide him so he cannot see as he walks around the circuit of the heavens?'

"Truly I tell you, our enemies will be totally destroyed, and what will be left of them, fire will consume! Settle with him and have peace. That way, good shall come to you. I tell you, receive instruction from his mouth, and place his words in your heart. If you return to the Almighty, you will be restored. If you put iniquity far from your tent and treat raw gold as dust, the fine gold of Ophir as the pebbles in the wadi, then the Almighty himself shall be your gold and your sparkling silver. For then you shall delight in the Almighty.

You shall lift up your face toward God. Entreat him, and he will hear you. What you decide shall succeed for you, and upon your ways sight shall shine. For the humble and downcast eyes he saves. He will deliver whoever is innocent, including you if your hands are clean."

Then Job answered and said, "Today especially, my complaint is bitter. His hand is heavy upon me in my groaning. If only I could find and see him, I could come to his holy dwelling! I would set out my case before him, fill my mouth with arguments, learn the words he would answer me, and understand what he would say to me. Would he then contend against me with his great power? No, he himself would heed me. There an upright man might argue with him, and I would once and for all be delivered from my judge. But if I go east, he is not there. West, I cannot perceive him. The north enfolds him where I cannot catch sight of him, and the south also hides him where I cannot see him.

"Yet he knows my way. If he tested me, I should come forth like gold. My foot has always walked in his steps. I have kept his way and have not turned aside. I have kept all the words of his mouth treasured in my heart and know no one can contradict him! He will carry out what he has in store for me. Thus, I am terrified before him. When I take thought, I dread him. For it is God who has made my heart faint, it's the Almighty who has terrified me. Yes, if I could only vanish in darkness and be hidden by the thick gloom before me. Why are the times not set by the Almighty? And why do his friends not see his days? Thieves remove landmarks. They steal herds and pasture them only for themselves. The donkeys of orphans they drive away and take the widows' ox for a small pledge. They force the needy off the road. All the poor of the land are driven into hiding.

"In the city, the dying groan, and the souls of the wounded cry out. Yet God does not see it as a disgrace! They are evil rebels against the light. They do not recognize his ways nor do they stay in his paths. When there is no light, the murderer rises to kill the poor and needy and, in the night, he acts like a thief. The eye of the adulterer watches for the twilight. He says, 'No eye shall see me.' He puts a mask over his face. In the dark, he breaks into homes. By day, he shuts himself in and does not know the light. Indeed for them, morning is deep darkness, and then they recognize the terrors of midnight. Now who can reduce my words to nothing and call me a liar?"

Then Bildad the Shuhite answered and said, "How can anyone be in the right against God? Or how can any born of woman be innocent? Even the moon is not bright, and the stars are not clean in his eyes. How much less a human being who is but a mortal, who is only a worm?"

Again, Job answered and said, "What help you give to the powerless, what strength to the feeble arm! How you give counsel to one without wisdom. How profuse is the advice you offer!"

Job took up his theme again and said, "As God lives, who takes away my right, the Almighty, who has made my life bitter? So long as I still have life and breath in me, the breath of God in my nostrils, my lips shall not speak any falsehood, nor my tongue utter deceit! Far be it from me to account you right. Until I die, I will never renounce my innocence. My justice I maintain, and I will not relinquish it!"

Then Zophar the Naamathite answered and said, "Indeed as for wisdom, no living creature can see her, no human can search her out. Where does she come from? Where is the place of understanding? She is hidden from the eyes of every living thing, even from the birds of the air she is concealed. Abaddon and Death say, 'Only by rumor have we heard of her.'

"But God understands the way to her. It is he alone who knows her place. For he beholds the ends of the earth and sees all that is under the heavens. When he weighed out the wind, measured out the waters, made a rule for the rain, and set a path for the thunderbolts, he saw wisdom and appraised her, established her, and searched her out. And to mortals he said, 'See: the fear of the Lord is wisdom and avoiding evil is understanding.'"

Job took up his theme again and said, "Oh that I were as in the months past, as in the days when God watched over me while he kept his lamp shining above my head, and by his light I walked through darkness. If it could only be like it was before, when I was in my flourishing days, when God sheltered my tent, when the Almighty was still with me. Whenever I went out to the gate of the city and took my seat in the square, the young men saw me and withdrew, the elders rose up and stood, the officials refrained from speaking, and the voice of the princes was silenced. The ear that heard blessed me, and the eye that saw acclaimed me.

"I rescued the poor who cried out for help, the orphans, and the unassisted. And the heart of the widow I made joyful, and the blessings of those ones in extremity came upon me. For me they listened and waited. They were silent for my counsel. They waited for me as for the rain and drank in my words like the spring rains. When I smiled on them, they could not believe it, and the light of my face, they would not let be dimmed. I lived like a king among the troops, like one who comforts mourners."

A young man named Elihu was standing behind them on the other end of the meadow with his arms folded over his chest and his back leaning against a tree. He kept listening to the four of them then started walking toward them.

Job continued on, "But now, those same people who are younger than I hold me in derision. Such strength as they had meant nothing to me. To me, they were like those banished from the community to dwell in caves of sand and stone. Yet now, they sing of me in mockery, I have become a byword among them. They do not hesitate to spit in my face, they plan my ruin, they trip my feet and tear up my path. I look for a helper to take up my cause, and there is none. They all say: 'What is this to us? This is your affair! Do we have to risk our life and limb for someone or something that has nothing to do with us?'

"No one is there for me! Amid the uproar, they seize in on me like waves and terrors roll over me. My dignity is driven off like the wind, and my well-being simply vanishes like a cloud. And now my life ebbs away from me, days of affliction have taken hold of me. At night in the darkness, they pierce my bones, and my sinews have no rest. With great difficulty, I change my clothes, the collar of my tunic fits around my waist. He allows them to cast me into the mire, and I have become like dust and ashes. I cry out to you, but you do not answer me. I stand, but you do not take notice. You have turned into my tormentor, and with your strong hand, you attack me. You raise me up and drive me before the wind. I am tossed about like the tempest. But should not a hand be held out for a wretched person in distress? Did I not weep for the hardships of others? Was my soul not grieved for the poor?

"But when I looked for good, evil came. When I expected light, darkness came. My inward parts seethe and will not be stilled, and days of affliction have overtaken me. I go about in gloom without the sun. I rise in the assembly and cry for help, but no one is there. My blackened skin falls away from me, and my very frame is scorched from the heat. My lyre is tuned to mourning, and my reed pipes to sounds of weeping. I made a covenant with my eyes not to gaze upon a virgin, yet no portion of God the Almighty on high comes to me. Does he not see my ways and number all my steps? If I have walked in falsehood, and my foot has hastened to deceit, let God weigh me in the scales of justice. Thus will he know my innocence!

"If my steps have turned out of the way, and my heart has followed my eyes, or any stain clings to my hands, then may I sow and another eat and may my produce be uprooted! If my heart lusted toward another woman, and I have lain in wait at her door, then let my wife grind for another, and may that other kneel over her! For that would be heinous, a crime to be condemned, a crime to fit the punishment of a fire that would come down to Abaddon till it consumed all my crops. If I have seen a wanderer without clothing or a poor man with no covering whose limbs have not blessed me when they were warmed with the fleece of my sheep, if I have raised my hand against the innocent because I saw that I had supporters at my gate—then may my arm fall from my own shoulder and my forearm be broken at the elbow!

"Had I put my trust in gold or called gold my majesty or rejoiced that my wealth was great and that I achieved it with my own hand or rejoiced over the destruction of my enemy or exulted when evil came upon him—all these things too would be crimes for condemnation. Oh, if I had one to hear my case, here is my signature: let the Almighty answer me! Let my accuser write out his indictment! Of all my steps, I should give him an account. If my land has cried out loud against me till its furrows wept together, if I have eaten without payment and grieved the hearts of its tenants, then let the thorns grow instead of wheat and stink weed instead of barley!"

Then the three men ceased to answer Job because in his own eyes he was in the right. But the anger of Elihu, son of Barachel the Buzite, of the clan of Ram was kindled. Looking down on the four of them from behind, he grew angry with Job for considering himself rather than God to be in the right. He was angry also with the three friends because they had not found a good answer and had not condemned Job. But since these four men were older than he, Elihu withheld his anger. But when Elihu saw that there was no reply from the three friends to Job concerning his latest summary of words, his wrath was inflamed.

So Elihu answered and said, as the four men turned around and looked at him, "I am young, and you are very old. Therefore I held back and was afraid to declare to you my knowledge. It is not those of many days who are wise nor the aged who understand the right. But it is a spirit, the breath of the Almighty in human beings that gives them understanding. So I say, listen to me: Behold, I have given ear to all of your arguments and have followed you attentively, yet none of you has convicted Job, not one could refute his stern statements. So do not say, 'We have met wisdom.'

"And to you, Job, I say you have said much in my hearing as I have listened to the sound of your words: I am clean, without transgression. I am innocent, there is no guilt in me. Yet he invents pretexts against me and counts me as his enemy. In this you are not just, for God is greater than mortals. Why then do you make complaint against him? For God does speak, once, even twice, though you do not see it, in dreams and in a vision of the night, when deep sleep falls upon mortals does he open their ears and terrify them with strong warnings. By this does he turn mortals from sin and keeps pride away from them. By this he holds man's soul from the pit, his life from passing to the grave. Or he will allow man to be chastened on a bed of pain and suffering to be continuous in his bones so that to his appetite, food is repulsive, his throat rejects the choicest nourishment. His soul draws near the pit, his life to the place of the dead.

Then he will take pity on him and say, 'Deliver him from going down into the pit. I have found for him a ransom.'

"Then his flesh shall become soft as a boy's. He shall be again as in the days of his youth. He shall pray, and God will favor him. He shall sing before all and say, 'I have sinned and did wrong, yet I was not punished accordingly. He delivered me from passing to the pit, and my life sees light.' And he shall see God's face with rejoicing, for he restores a person's righteousness. See, Job, be attentive and listen to me. All these things God does, two even three times for a man, bringing back his soul from the pit to the light, in the light of the living! Now if you have anything to say, then answer me. Speak out! I should like to see you rightly justified. If not, then be silent, and I will teach you wisdom."

Elihu went on, saying, "You who are wise and have knowledge, listen to me, hear my discourse. Let us choose what is right. Let us determine among ourselves what is good. For Job has said, 'I am innocent, but God has taken away what is my right. I declare the judgment on me to be a lie, and my arrow wound is incurable, sinless though I am.' What man is like Job? But I say, you are just as bad when you drink in blasphemies like water, keep company with evildoers, go along with the wicked, then dare to say, 'There is no profit in pleasing God.' Therefore you who have understanding, hear me: God requites mortals for their conduct and brings home to them their way of life. Surely God cannot act wickedly nor prevent justice. Who gave him charge over the earth? Or who set all the world in its place?

"If he were to set his mind to it and gather to himself his spirit and breath, all flesh would perish together, and mortals would return to dust. So how can you condemn the supreme Just One? I tell you there is no darkness so dense that evildoers can hide in it. No one has God set a time to come before him in judgment. Without inquiry, he shatters the mighty and appoints others in their place. Thus he discerns their works and, overnight, they are crushed. Where the wicked are, he strikes them down in a place where all can see because they turned away from him and did not understand his ways at all and made the cry of the poor reach him. So let Job be tested to the limit, since his answers are those of the impious. For he is adding rebellion to his sin by brushing off our arguments and addressing many words to God."

Elihu continued on, saying, "Do you think it right to say, 'I am right, not God?' It is idle to say that God does not hear? Or that the Almighty does not take notice? And, further, I tell you: The case is before him. With trembling you should wait upon him. But now that you have done otherwise, God's anger punishes nor does he show much concern over your life. Yet Job, to no purpose, opens his mouth, multiplying words without knowledge."

Elihu continued, saying, "God is great, not disdainful. His strength of purpose is great. He does not preserve the life of the wicked. He rather establishes the right of the poor and does not divert his eyes from the just. He also seats them on thrones with kings, exalted forever. But if he bounds them with fetters, held fast by bonds of affliction, he lets them know what they have done and how arrogant are their sins. He opens their eyes to correction and tells them to turn back from evil. If they listen and serve him, they prosper forever in happiness. But if they do not listen, they pass to the grave and perish for lack of knowledge.

"Though you are full of the judgment of the wicked, judgment and justice will be maintained. Let not anger at abundance entice you nor great bribery lead you astray. Do not long for the night when people vanish to their places. Be careful not to turn to evil, for this you have preferred over affliction. Look, God is exalted in his power. What teacher is there like him? Who prescribes for him his way? Who tells him, 'You have done wrong'? Remember, you should extol his work, which people have praised in song. All humankind beholds it. Everyone views it from afar. See, God is great beyond our knowledge, the number of his years past searching out. He holds in check the waterdrops that filter in rain from his flood till the clouds flow with them, and they rain down on all humankind. For by all this he judges the nations and gives food in abundance. In his hand, he holds the lightning and commands it to strike the mark. His thunder announces him and incites the fury of the storm.

"At this my heart trembles and leaps out of its place. Listen to his angry voice and the rumble that comes forth from his mouth! Truly his voice roars, his majestic voice thunders. God thunders forth marvels with his voice. He does great things beyond our knowing. He says to the snow, 'Fall to the earth.' He says the same to his heavy drenching rain. He shuts up all humankind indoors so that all people may know his work. The wild beasts take to cover and remain quiet in their dens. He brings the tempest forth as well as the cool wind from the north and the warm wind from the south. He changes their rounds according to his plans.

"All this, whether for punishment or mercy, he causes to come to pass. See, Job, stand and consider the marvels of God! Do you know how he does all this? So I say to you, 'Behold the marvels of him who is perfect in knowledge.' From Zaphon, the golden splendor comes forth, surrounding God's awesome majesty! He is the Almighty! He remains preeminent in power and judgment, abundant in justice, who never oppresses."

At this point, Job and the other four men gathered up their food and water and continued on their way through the desert, back to the castle.

Now, several miles to the northeast of the castle in the middle of the mountains, several hundred Sabeans were galloping at full speed on horseback toward the castle. They gathered at least four hundred fresh troops from southern Arabia and were returning to challenge the Chaldeans for the castle. The leader, Lucius, came to the top of a high mountain, stopped, and looked down. He signaled the others behind him to stop. He could see all the Chaldeans down below, walking in and out of the castle, and the leaders partying, eating, drinking, and laughing outside on the terrace. Lucius's face turned red, and he said to the party behind him, "Our time has finally come! This is the day we've all been waiting for! Now we'll make them pay for taking away what we had first." He turned his horse around and galloped in front of his troops, then down the dusty road.

He began to blow a war cry through a horn, and all the rest of his troops galloped and stormed down the road at full speed behind him, all ready for a fight, screaming and geared up for battle. They all galloped down the road, then along the northwest side of the lake, then through the grassy fields and, finally, out on to the plantation. They stormed over the plantation, toward the mountains at the southwest. The Chaldeans heard the sound of thunder. They all rose up, looked out, and saw the Sabeans riding over the plantation, toward the mountains. The Sabeans stopped and turned their horses around with their backs toward the hills and facing the castle. They arranged themselves into four rows, each one behind the other and all consisting of about a hundred troops per row. Lucius rode out a few steps into the field, stopped, and again, blew the sound of a war cry through his horn.

The Chaldeans watched from high upon the northeast mountain where the castle sat. They said, "Well, it looks like the Sabeans are back. And they want to take back the castle." They laughed and said, "The fools! They're now challenging us? They've regrouped."

One soldier said, "I knew someday they would do this and return."

Their leader, Ito, a fierce warrior who at birth had been adopted into the Chaldean clan screamed back, "Shut up! No! Never! We'll never run from them! All of you now hear this. We are not cowards! We are gods! We are warriors! We defeated them before! We will easily do it again! Gather the troops, all of them, and sound the war cry!"

So all the troops gathered together and formed a battle plan of their own. They put on their shields, took hold of all their swords and spears, jumped on their horses, and galloped full speed over the terrace, down the road, then along the northwest side of the lake, out over the grassy fields, and then with a huge raging dust storm behind them and with the sound of thunder multiplied several times, out on to the plantation. Ito screamed back to his troops behind him, "We'll meet and take them head on and drive those dirty lowlifes back into the dust where they came from!"

They continued the charge even faster and, again, at Ito's command, all raised their spears and swords. But just then, Lucius thought to himself, *Wait, I have a personal grudge against this Ito. I want him for myself. I won't rest until I can personally slit his throat.* He thought, *If I get off my horse and raise my sword to him, he will stop his armies and come alone to me and see what I want, if only out of curiosity if nothing else. And he will not send all his armies onto one lone man either. It's a gamble but one I must take.* So Lucius told his armies to hold back and wait.

They said, "But no, General, they will kill you!

He said, "No, do as I say!" He took his sword, got off of his horse, and walked out a few hundred yards to meet the Chaldeans' charging troops alone. As they got closer, Lucius held his sword up with his right hand, high into the air. As the Chaldeans continued the charge, Lucius closed his eyes tight, kept holding up the sword, and began to sweat. His troops behind him were growing increasingly nervous and anxious to charge back at the Chaldeans. Lucius heard the thundering sound of galloping horses suddenly begin to decrease, then stop altogether. He opened his eyes and saw the whole army of Chaldeans about three hundred yards in front of him, standing still, holding their spears and swords erect, and trying to calm their horses. The Chaldeans arranged their troops of about 550 in the same way as the Sabeans had arranged theirs—in five rows of about one hundred right behind each other. Lucius then motioned to Ito with his sword to get off his horse and come to him in the middle of all the troops.

Ito got down off his horse hesitantly, pulled his sword out, held it high in the air, and walked out into the opening, and stood face-to-face with Lucius only about a foot in front of him. Lucius lifted his sword high into the air, issuing a personal challenge to Ito. Ito raised his sword also and hit Lucius's with it. Everyone heard clearly the echoing sound of metal clanging together, and both sides grew more nervous and anxious. Then Lucius lowered his sword and, in a second, sliced Ito's throat from his left ear to his right. Immediately blood poured out onto the ground as Ito screamed and fell dead to the ground. The Chaldeans screamed in anger and rage, pulled out their swords, and all charged straight on. They ran over and trampled Lucius to death and went right for the Sabeans who also sounded their war cry and charged straight back at them. Both armies clashed head on, right into each other.

Although there were more Chaldeans than Sabeans, and the Chaldeans were by far stronger, more powerful, and more experienced at warfare than the Sabeans, a lot of the Chaldeans were half drunk and in a silly mood; whereas the Sabeans were all fresh from training and in a much better frame of mind for a fight. This made the odds much more even.

Then hundreds of arrows and spears all went flying through the air from the Chaldeans army to the Sabeans; then from the Sabeans army to the Chaldeans as both sides opened a vicious and violent attack on each other. As the war cries grew louder, the Chaldeans began throwing their swords straight out and stabbing the Sabeans directly in the throat with them. In a rage, the vengeful Sabeans continued running on horseback and slamming directly into the Chaldeans army; all swinging their swords wildly with all their might and knocking the half-intoxicated Chaldeans off of their horses, then trampling them under the feet of their horses. The Sabeans continued swinging their swords in a frenzy and slicing them right into the sides of the necks of the Chaldeans. Anger and pure rage blazed in each one of the Sabeans minds as they all continued their violent attack on the Chaldeans, swinging their swords, slicing the Chaldeans necks, killing, even beheading them, and knocking them off of their horses.

Now the Chaldeans realized that they had completely underestimated the Sabeans. So the Chaldean's army clashed directly into the Sabean's, knocking many of them off of their horses. They, too, then pulled out their swords and began swinging them, counterattacking against the Sabeans, stabbing and beheading them. Many dead bodies were falling lifelessly off horses and being trampled underfoot. One Chaldean soldier raised a spear and hurdled it down as hard as he could, right into the leg of a Sabean. The Sabean screamed and clutched his leg. The startled Chaldean soldier's horse screamed and rose upright on its hind legs. As it came down forward, it smashed right onto the head of the Sabean soldier, sending his dead body and his horse crashing to the ground.

The ear-splitting sounds of battle cries and of steel hitting together could be heard high up into the mountains as all the soldiers from both sides continued on and on, sword fighting on horseback, and throwing arrows and spears back and forth at each other. But these swords and spears kept bouncing off the armored shields that both the Chaldeans and Sabeans wore around their chests and abdomens.

The Sabeans continued on relentlessly, trying with full force to thrust themselves through the Chaldeans army and make their way to the castle straight ahead. But the Chaldeans continued with all their strength to hold them back. One of the Chaldean soldiers blew a deafening war cry through his mouth horn into the air, and they all again charged at full speed directly into the Sabeans. The Chaldeans again continued swinging their swords violently, beheading the Sabeans and knocking them off of their horses. They lost all control of their wits and continued on and on for several minutes, slamming and crashing into the Sabeans, slicing their necks, stabbing them in the legs, and sending them dead to the ground. They all began laughing and screaming in delight as they continued their onslaught into the Sabeans, knocking them off of their horses and trampling them underfoot. Now the Sabeans realized that well over half of their army was gone; as the barbaric Chaldeans kept charging right into them at full speed and never showing any sign of letting up.

Then two Sabeans on horseback were forming a plan. While the Chaldeans were killing off many of the Sabeans in an obsessive and bloody rage, the one Sabean soldier took half of what was left of their army and led them out into the open field, several hundred feet to the right, while the other Sabean soldier with the other half of their army kept the Chaldeans busy so they would not notice and was leading them forward away from the castle toward the forest. While the Chaldeans continued over and over to slaughter the Sabeans and their horses, the Sabeans never let down their guard. They fought back and kept up the struggle valiantly, throwing spears and swords back at the Chaldeans, killing and slaying some of them as well, while moving backward still toward the forest, making believe that the Chaldeans were pushing them back.

The other half of the Sabean army galloped full speed straight ahead, then all turned around to the left in a semicircle and charged again full speed toward their rival Chaldeans from behind. They pounced on the Chaldeans, slamming full force into their horses from behind. The Chaldeans screamed and panicked. They were unable to control their horses as they were jumping up on their hind legs. Many of the Chaldeans went tumbling off backward and getting killed by the stampede of frightened horses. The Sabean army continued pouncing and slamming into the Chaldeans from behind. Many jumped off their horses, onto the backs of the Chaldeans on their horses, and went on a killing spree, stabbing the Chaldeans in the back of the neck and head, slicing their swords into their necks, and pushing them off of their horses. The horses screamed and continued to panic, running in all different directions while killing Chaldeans as well as Sabeans.

The Sabean army from the front then began slamming and charging into the Chaldean army. Again, they were throwing swords and spears straight ahead, stabbing many of the Chaldeans to death. Both armies of Sabeans in front and back of the Chaldean's rammed into them simultaneously, slaughtering them in a bloody violent rage. Both of the Sabean armies leaped off their horses, onto the backs of the Chaldean's horses, and attacked the Chaldeans with all their might. They all continued stabbing and slicing into them with their spears and swords and killing them with their fists as well. In the chaos and confusion of war, many more Chaldeans as well as Sabeans fell from their horses, onto the ground, and were killed by the horses.

Now there were more Sabeans than Chaldeans. Neither side had any spears or swords left. The Sabeans grew overconfident and charged after the Chaldeans, driving them all into the woods.

The Chaldeans all ran deep into the forest, into the dense thick woods where the Sabeans could not go with horses. The Sabeans sat on the edge of the forest on their horses and laughed at the fleeing Chaldeans, saying, "Look at them, they were so much stronger, and there were so many more! Yet look at them now running from the weaker army like scared rabbits!"

Another Sabean soldier said, "We used our brains! And brains can overpower bulk anytime!"

Deep in the forest, the Chaldeans fell down on the ground, totally exhausted. They looked up at the trees and began to break small branches off of them and pick up sticks from the ground. They tore parts of their clothes off and wrapped them around the tops of the sticks and branches, then ran back to the edge of the forest.

The Sabeans saw them running out of the forest, toward them, dragging lit torches on the ground, and setting the grass on fire. They lifted the torches and threw them up at the Sabeans and down on the grass all around them and started a huge grass fire. The Sabeans leaped off of their horses and seized the Chaldeans, beating them up. But the Chaldeans fought back with all their strength. A violent fistfight between the two armies ensued. Then they all picked up swords and spears from the ground and went after each other on foot. They continued tearing and slicing into each other; tearing one another apart, sword fighting and fist-fighting, throwing lit torches at each other, and killing each other with brutal and savage drive and determination right down to the last two men.

Job and his four friends were still walking back to the castle. They hiked up a mountain, then stopped at the top to catch their breath. While resting, Job looked straight ahead and saw in a vast distance his castle still sitting on the rocky hill. As they walked down the front side of the mountain toward the plantation, they all could hear the clamor of some kind of great disturbance or commotion; horses bellowing out in panic and the screams and war cries of an intense battle. As they continued their trek down the hill, it grew louder. They reached the bottom, ran through the forest, then on to the plantation.

As they walked out on to the open fields, they heard nothing but quiet. The battle was over. They saw all the dead bodies of the soldiers, both the Sabeans and the Chaldeans as well as their horses lying all over the ground. Then they saw all the rest of the horses in a herd, running off together toward the south. Then over by the lake, they saw a strange obelisk shaped tower extending from the ground over twenty meters tall. They walked over to it and saw on the very top a stone head and face of a pagan idol with two huge blue mirrorlike eyes. Job said very solemnly, "It's an image of the Leviathan, the giant beast from the bottom of this very lake that once tried to devour my wife, Sitidos, and I before we were rescued by the mighty Ziz. The Sabeans or the Chaldeans must have erected it. They probably prayed to it and worshipped it as a god. But it's a pagan idol. It must come down at once!"

Job turned and looked out into the fields and again gazed at all the dead bodies lying hacked to pieces. He sat down with a broken heart and said, "My Lord and my God! Is it too much to ask you? Why have you permitted all of this to happen? It's true all these people were my enemies, yes. But why have you let me see so much evil? It seems that nothing but death and destruction and heartbreak are all around me. Was it really necessary to allow me to see and experience all of this?"

Then the five men, for just a moment, felt the shaking of a great earthquake and endured the force of a mighty wind. As the wind grew stronger, hurtling them all to the ground, they saw a gigantic whirlwind-like tornado sweeping across the plantation at a speed none of them had ever seen and heading straight for them. It struck the dead bodies and scattered them all high into the air then to the four corners of the earth. As it was almost upon them, all five men fell face first to the ground, trembling in terror.

Then the voice of the Lord God thundered from it and spoke, "Job! Job, my child! Yes, you have seen much evil, death, and destruction and have endured and experienced much injustice. But you've also seen and experienced much mercy, holiness, and goodness as well. I have slain all of your enemies for you as I have promised, and yet you still raise complaint and are sad. Why?"

Quivering and on the verge of fainting, Job responded to the Lord, "But I never wanted them nor anyone to die so horribly and violently. Even though they were my enemies, I still weep for them."

The Lord then answered, "Job, by saying this, you have proven yourself to be a being of great mercy, forgiveness, and compassion. This will be well-remembered of you on your day of judgment."

Then, again, the Lord spoke to Job out of the storm and said, "But I still must ask you this, who are you to darken counsel with all those words of ignorance you have so firmly spoken? Who are you to say you are right and not God?" Then the Lord cast a deep sleep on Job's three friends: Eliphaz, Bildad, and Zophar. He then dismissed

Elihu from their company who immediately rose up and journeyed back to his homeland.

Then Job could hear nothing. He rose up, looked around, and saw nothing but his three childhood friends sleeping on the ground. Then, out of nowhere, he again heard the voice of the Lord, saying, "Job, arise. Gird up your loins now, like a man. I will question you, and you tell me the answers!"

Job arose, looked to the south and saw the largest living creature he had ever seen, even larger than the Leviathan. It was a huge mammoth covered with long gray and white woolly fur. Two enormous white tusks protruded upward in a semi-circle position from its face. An enormously long trunk sprung from its nose, which it was using to pull fruit and branches off of trees to eat. It could easily look over the roof of a three-story building. It seemed very docile to Job, just standing there, eating in peace. Still, to see something on land that huge and alive at the same time sent a chill of overwhelming terror through his body.

While casually chewing its food, the living monstrosity turned to its left and looked straight down at Job. Job was so terrified he collapsed onto the ground. But the Lord woke him up and said, "Behold the Behemoth. But do not be frightened. It will do you no harm. It does not eat meat but only fruit and grazes on the grass of the fields. And, further, I tell you, it will come to your defense when you experience your greatest trial of all. And to me, it's merely a puppy or kitten on a leash."

In less than a second, the Lord fixed Job's feet onto the back of the Behemoth's neck and whisked him high into the air amongst the stars, through the heavens, and showed him all the kingdoms of the earth and all that he had created.

Then God put these questions to Job, "Where were you when I founded the earth? Tell me if you have any understanding. Who determined its size? Surely you know? Who stretched out the measuring line for it? Who laid its cornerstone while the morning stars sang together and all the sons of God shouted for joy? Who shut within doors the sea when it burst forth from the womb, when I made the clouds its garments and thick darkness its swaddling bands?

Or where were you when I set limits for it and fastened the bar of its door, and said, 'Thus shall you come but no further and here shall your proud waves stop?'

"Have you ever, in your lifetime, commanded the morning and shown the dawn its place? Or taken hold of the ends of the earth till the wicked are shaken from it? The earth is changed as clay by the sea and dyed like a garment. But from the wicked, their light is withheld, and the arm of pride is shattered. Have you ever entered into the sources of the sea or walked about on the bottom of the deep? Have the gates of death been shown to you? Or have you seen the gates of darkness? Have you comprehended the breadth of the earth? Tell me if you know it all. What is the way to the dwelling of light, and darkness—where is its place?"

The Lord continued on, "Tell me, have you entered the storehouses of the snow and seen the storehouses of the hail, which I have reserved for times of distress, for a day of war and battle? And what is the way to the parting of the winds, where the east wind spreads over the earth? Who has laid out a channel for the downpour and a path for the thunderstorm to bring rain to uninhabited lands and the wildernesses, to drench the desolate wasteland till the desert blooms with verdure? Has the rain a father? Who has begotten the drops of dew? Out of whose womb comes the ice, and who gives the hoarfrost its birth in the skies when the waters all lie covered as though with stone that holds captive the surface of the deep?

"Have you tied cords to the Pleiades? Or loosened the bonds of Orion? Can you bring forth the Mazzaroth in their season? Or guide the bear with her cubs? Do you know the ordinances of the great heavens? Can you put into effect their plan on the earth? Can you raise your voice to the clouds for them to cover you with a deluge of waters? Can you send forth the lightnings on their way so that they say to you, 'Here we are'? Who tilts the water jars of heaven so that the dust of the earth will be changed into a mass of life-giving water? Who provided nourishment to the raven when its young cry out to God for food?"

The Lord God continued on, "Do you know when the mountain goats are born or know when the birth pangs of deer come? Do you give the horse his strength or clothe his neck with a mane? Yet he charges into battle, has no fear, and does not retreat from the sword. Even from afar, he senses the battle, the roar of the officers, and the shouting. Is it by your understanding that the hawk soars and spreads his wings toward the south? Does the eagle fly up at your command to build his nest up high? Do you choose on which cliff he is to dwell and spend the night? His young ones greedily drink blood. Where the slain are, there is he. Have you, Job, planned all this?"

Then the Lord again went on, "Will one who argues with the Almighty be corrected? Let him who would instruct God give answer!"

Then Job answered the Lord and said, "Look, I am of little account. What can I answer you? I put my hand over my mouth. I have spoken once, I will not reply. Twice, but I will do so no more."

Again, the Lord answered Job and said, "Again, I say, gird up your loins now like a man. I will question you, and you tell me the answers! Would you refuse to acknowledge my right? Would you condemn me that you may be justified? Have you an arm like God? Or can you thunder with a voice like his? Can you adorn yourself with great grandeur and majesty and clothe yourself with glory and splendor? Can you let loose the fury of your wrath, look at everyone who is proud, and bring them down and humble them? Can you tear down the wicked in their place and bury them in the dust and then hide them in their prison cells? If you can do all this, then I will praise you, for your own right hand can save you."

The Lord said to Job, "Again, I say to you: Behold the Behemoth, whom your very feet even now are standing on and whom I made along with you, who feeds on grass like an ox. See the strength in his loins, the power in the sinews of his belly. He moveth his tail like a cedar. The sinews of his thighs are like cables. His bones are like tubs of bronze. His limbs are like iron rods. He is the first of God's ways, only his Maker can approach him with a sword. Under lotus trees he lies, in coverts of the reedy swamp. The lotus trees give him shade in the heat of the day, and all about him are the poplars in the wadi. If the river grows violent, he is not disturbed. He is tranquil though the

Jordan surges about his mouth. Who can capture him by his eyes or pierce his nose with a trap?"

The Lord continued asking Job, "Can you lead the great Leviathan, the beast who nearly devoured you, about with a hook? Or tie down his tongue with a rope? Can you pierce his nose or cheek with a ring or gaff? Will he then plead with you, time after time, or address you with tender words? Will he make a covenant with you that you may have him as a slave forever? Can you play with him as with a bird or dog? But once you lay a hand upon him, no need to recall any other conflict."

The Lord continued to Job, "Whoever might vainly hope to do so need only see him to be overthrown. No one is fierce enough to arouse him. Who then dares stand before me? Whoever has assailed me, I will pay back! Everything under the heavens is mine. I need hardly mention his limbs, his strength, and the fitness of his equipment. Who can strip off his outer garment or penetrate his double armor? Who can force open his mouth? Or who has the courage to get close to his terrible teeth? Rows of scales are on his back so tightly sealed and fitted together that no air can come between them. When he sneezes, light flashes forth. His eyes are like the eyelids of dawn. Out of his mouth go forth torches, sparks of fire leap forth. From his nostrils comes smoke as from a seething pot or bowl. His breath sets coals afire. A flame comes from his mouth.

"Strength abides in his neck, and power leaps before him. His heart is cast as hard as stone, cast as the lower millstone. When he rises up, the gods are afraid. When he crashes down, they fall back. Should a sword reach him, it will not avail, nor will spear, dart, or javelin. He regards iron as chaff and bronze as rotten wood. No arrow will put him to flight. Slingstones used against him are but straw as are clubs. He laughs at the crash of a spear. Under him are sharp pottery fragments spreading a threshing sledge upon the mire. He makes the depth boil like a pot. He makes the sea like a perfume bottle. Behind him, he leaves a shining path. Upon the earth, there is none like him. He was made fearless. He looks over all who are haughty. He is king over all proud beasts. And you are just a little man. So how dare you doubt and question me so?"

Then the Lord God returned Job to the earth, and the Behemoth was nowhere in sight. Then Job fell to the ground and worshipped God. He repented of all that he had said and answered the Lord, saying, "I know that you can do all things, and that there is no purpose of yours that can be hindered. Who is this who obscures counsel with such ignorance? I have spoken but did not understand, things too marvelous for me, which I did not know. Listen, and I will speak. I will put the questions to you, and you tell me the answers. By hearsay I had heard of you, but now my eye has seen you. Therefore I disown what I have said and repent in dust and ashes."

By now Job was nearly asleep on the ground under the shade and comfort of the forest trees. The Leviathan was floating just under the surface of the lake with only the top of its head, its eyes and nose above the surface, watching Job who was nearly asleep. Job vaguely heard a light splashing in the water which, at first, only annoyed him. Then came a tremendous upsurge of water from the lake. Two giant columns of water arose, then fell backward, revealing the Leviathan's scaled blue and green hide. Its long neck sprung forward up out of the water straight ahead, causing a shower of water to fall on Job. Job woke up, but because he was so tired, still had his eyes closed and thought he was having a dream. He sensed darkness overcoming him, then heard a loud thumping on the ground.

The shadow of Leviathan's long neck kept rising higher and higher on the shore until it reached the tree Job was sleeping under and then totally engulfed him. He finally woke up and looked up in the air. To his horror and shock, he saw the hideous beast gazing down at him with its eyes blazing brightly in the morning sunlight. Job jumped to his feet, screamed in terror, and ran as fast as he could the other way into the forest. Then he felt the force of a powerful earthquake. All around him, the ground was splitting and cracking apart, causing him to run out into the open. The quaking became more and more powerful and intense while the ground continued splitting in several smaller sections. As he tried to maintain his balance, Job would not dare look behind him and was thinking the whole time that it was being caused by Leviathan.

Then with the most powerful crashing of all, the Behemoth's front left foot hit the ground right in front of Job, heaving him into the air, then back down on the ground. Lying on his back, stunned and bewildered, Job opened his eyes and looked straight up. He first saw the Behemoth's enormous upward curved tusks high in the air, then its head chest and legs, all looming directly over him. Then, to his left, high above him at almost the same height of the Behemoth's head, he plainly saw the Leviathan's head and neck come into view. Job watched from the ground, paralyzed with fear as both giants roared and lashed out at each other with him in the middle. They began slamming and crashing their immense bodies into each other, butting heads, and with full force, trying to push the other one back. Again, Job screamed in horror, rolled out of the way, rose to his feet, and ran as fast as he could out on to the open plantation.

The Behemoth was obviously a lot bigger, more massive and powerful than Leviathan. With its tremendous size, strength, and weight, it could easily bring Leviathan down and crush all of its bones and drive it into the ground. But with Leviathan's six-inch-long dagger-like teeth, razor-sharp talons and horns, and four upward spikes extending from the tip of its tail, it could easily tear into Behemoth, slice its flesh to ribbons, and mortally wound it.

Job watched, spellbound, as both giants continued on slamming head first into each other; pressing their feet into the ground for leverage, and each emitting roars of anger and rage while desperately trying to push the other one back. At this, the Behemoth excelled. With its massive bulk and weight, it managed to push the Leviathan backward, all the way to the shore of the lake. It let go of its smaller rival, took a few steps back, raised its enormous powerful trunk, and smashed it right down on the back of Leviathan's head and neck.

Again, Behemoth pulled back, swung its trunk, and delivered a powerful blow to the left side of Leviathan's head. With several more hard blows from Behemoth's powerful trunk, Leviathan began screaming and crying out in pain and bewilderment. Again, Behemoth raised its powerful trunk high into the air and dropped it full force on top of Leviathan. Once again, Behemoth delivered a fast and powerful blow with its trunk on top of Leviathan, sending it crashing face first to the ground. Now Behemoth had Leviathan at his feet and continued over and over, clubbing and beating all over him while Leviathan continued screaming and roaring, trying to escape. Then Leviathan managed to rise to its feet, lower its head, and thrust its horns from the top of its head into Behemoth's chest. Behemoth screamed in pain, and Leviathan pulled its horns back out as blood poured forth from Behemoth's wounds.

Again, Leviathan lowered its head, ran straight ahead, and stabbed both horns directly up into Behemoth's throat. Once again, Behemoth let out an ear-piercing cry, raised its head, then crashed it along with its trunk and tusks, straight down on Leviathan. Leviathan tore its horns out of Behemoth's throat and again fell to the ground as more blood poured out of Behemoth. Behemoth was wounded, but he still had plenty of strength left in him, for the wounds were not that deep. Leviathan rose to his feet again, and again, they clashed. Again, the Behemoth rose its trunk and continued delivering one powerful blow after another on top of Leviathan's head, back, and neck. Then Behemoth lowered its head, and with all of its strength, hit Leviathan in the chest with its trunk and sent him reeling backward, into the lake.

Angered and enraged, Leviathan jumped out of the lake, onto the ground, and charged full speed toward Behemoth. The Behemoth ran back toward him, hitting Leviathan as hard as he could, again sending him reeling backward into the lake. Behemoth charged into the lake after him and continued his assault on Leviathan, pummeling into him with his entire body and dunking him into the water with its huge massive front feet, trying to drown him. Then Behemoth rose up on its hind legs and came down into the water with all its weight, right on top of Leviathan, sending him to the bottom.

But now, fortunately for the Leviathan, the water absorbed most of the impact. Leviathan heaved its entire body up out of the water, crashing head first into Behemoth but barely budged him. Again, Leviathan leaped straight ahead at Behemoth and sunk its teeth into his face. Then Leviathan dug all of its talons from its two front feet into Behemoth's hide. Behemoth trumpeted a scream that seemed as if it could be heard from miles away as more blood gushed out of him. Leviathan swung its powerful tail out of the water to the right, sending its four tail spikes right into the Behemoth's left side, causing still more blood to pour out. Again, Behemoth wailed out a trumpet sound and, with all its strength, pushed Leviathan backward into the water again. Once again, Leviathan charged out of the water at Behemoth, and Behemoth charged as fast as he could toward Leviathan. Again, in uncontrollable anger and rage, both slammed head first into each other.

They continued butting heads at full force like two enraged mountain rams, desperately trying to push each other backward, and each one trying to knock the other one to the ground while emitting deafening roars and cries of defiance toward the other. Behemoth took a few steps backward, then ran as fast as he could, attacked Leviathan by slamming his entire body into him, and again knocked him backward into the lake. But Leviathan retaliated by charging out of the water, straight at Behemoth, and once again, both clashed head on. Like two wild and vicious animals, they continued lashing out at each other—the Behemoth swinging its long and powerful trunk out at Leviathan, striking him continuously in the face and head, while the Leviathan continued retaliating by swinging its long and powerful neck at Behemoth and snapping its jaws viciously at him.

With a deafening high-pitched roar, the Leviathan opened its jaws as wide as he could, pulled its body back, then thrust it forward with all its might, and clamped its teeth down as hard as it could around Behemoth's neck. But nothing happened. A second time, Leviathan bit down hard around Behemoth's neck. But this time, blood poured from his neck as the gigantic mastodon let out a stentorian scream of pain. He again administered several powerful blows onto Leviathan's back and head with its trunk and massive front legs, finally knocking him to the ground. But Leviathan managed to rise to its feet and attack Behemoth again with its horns, teeth, and talons, as both again lashed out viciously at each other in a battle to the death.

As the battle raged on across the plantation, Job watched with both eyes wide open while feeling like his heart was about to pound out of his chest. While the gargantuan combatants were coming closer to him, Job turned and ran for his life, toward the southeast where the plantation gave way to a hillside. Then he stopped, gasped for his breath, and turned around.

Then with all the power in his body, Behemoth drove Leviathan backward into the lake waters. Leviathan then opened its huge jaws and breathed out its gigantic flame of fire straight ahead on Behemoth, driving him backward onto the land and into a small wooded area. Behemoth then shook its head and charged full speed straight toward his foe. But Leviathan stopped him dead in his tracks with another powerful blast of his flaming breath. Behemoth charged at Leviathan again and again. Leviathan let out another blast of fire and lit the ground on fire in front of him. Behemoth took several steps backward, inhaled, and at full force, exhaled a powerful blast of wind out of his trunk, straight down on to the fire, hence, extinguishing it.

As Behemoth charged forward again, Leviathan stepped back and, again, set the ground on fire with his flaming breath. Again, Behemoth stopped, plunged its trunk into the water and inhaled again, filling the entire inside of its trunk with water. Behemoth stood erect, pointed its trunk forward, and exhaled the water all over the fire, extinguishing it yet again. Leviathan backed up into the water until the entire back half of its body was submerged under the calm waves. He then let out an ear-piercing scream and exhaled another blast of fire, this time straight ahead at Behemoth. Once again, Behemoth took a deep breath, rose up, and exhaled a fountain of water through the air at full force, straight ahead, hitting Leviathan's stream of fire, weakening it, and turning it into mere smoke. Behemoth began moving and swinging its head and body vigorously from side to side as he sprayed the water out of his trunk and showered the entire area in water. Then, again, he sprayed it straight ahead directly into Leviathan's mouth, extinguishing the fire completely.

Behemoth then charged full speed into the water after Leviathan and, again, slammed right into him. Leviathan continued stabbing its horns into the giant Behemoth's trunk and face, drawing more blood and trying repeatedly to bring him down. Leviathan lowered its head into the water and stabbed its horns into Behemoth's front legs. Then he lifted his tail out of the water, swung it high into the air to the right, then stabbed the four protruding spikes on the end of it into Behemoth's left side. He wrenched the tail spikes back out again, tearing out clumps of flesh and fur, then stabbed them back into the wound as blood spilled into the water. Blood also poured out of Behemoth's front legs and oozed through the water. Behemoth let out a scream of rage and, again, gained the upper hand. He began trouncing Leviathan's body with its powerful front legs and feet, plunging Leviathan deeper into the water and onto the floor of the lake, trying to crush him.

As a nearly breathless Job watched the unparalleled spectacle, he was suddenly startled. Sticking in the ground and quivering beside him was a shining silver metal sword. He looked up and saw about a hundred feet in front of him, Zerah, standing and gazing directly at him with that all too familiar evil stare. Again, Satan's low, blood-curdling voice spoke to Job through Zerah's mouth, saying, "You thought you won. That you saw the last of me? Never! As I said in the beginning, I refuse to worship and obey God. I'm Satan. All powerful! And all evil! And I won't rest until I kill you and take your wretched and stinking soul to the icy, fire-laden depths of hell with me." Zerah let out a loud evil laugh as a sword appeared in his left hand. He ran straight for Job with the sword pointing straight ahead and, again, screamed, "Let's see what you can do!"

Job pulled the sword out of the ground to defend himself. Zerah was nearly upon him, swinging his sword wildly. Job lifted his sword up in front of him, again, only to defend himself, but in a second, found himself in a full-fledged sword fight against the same evil enemy incarnate that killed his friend, Aram. The once despised diseased and humiliated old man whom everyone totally rejected was now fighting heroically for his life. Although Job fought valiantly, he not only knew that he was losing but that Zerah was going easy on him, playing some sort of a mind game with him. He saw an evil smile crack Zerah's ice-cold face.

As the duel raged on, Zerah was pushing Job backward toward a hillside. Just then, Leviathan bit down hard on Behemoth's trunk and hung on. Behemoth once again screamed in pain and ran backward, out of the water. He lifted his trunk and slammed Leviathan onto the ground. But Leviathan would not let go. The giant, Behemoth, swung his trunk to his right at full force and sent his reptilian adversary crashing onto the ground in front of the pagan tower. Both giants were badly wounded. Leviathan was lying on the ground, nearly unconscious and beaten to a pulp, while Behemoth was stabbed and bitten numerous times as a continuous stream of blood flowed down his trunk. But both continued lashing out at each other, each hellbent on bringing the other one down.

The human sword fight raged on to a fever pitch as well as Zerah continued pushing Job backward, while the two primeval giants continued their battle to the death. The sun was now in just the right spot in the sky where its rays touched the glassy eyes of the pagan idol, which sat on top of the tower. Two bright orange laser beam-like rays shot out of the eyes in a downward direction, into the mirrorlike eyes of the Leviathan. Leviathan lifted his head and then reflected the rays directly at Behemoth, singeing his fur and hide. Behemoth screamed and retreated backward a few steps. Again, the sun's rays touched the eyes of the pagan idol on top of the tower, which again were reflected downward and were absorbed into Leviathan's eyes. Again, he sent them back at Behemoth, burning his fur and skin. Leviathan screeched loudly and attacked Behemoth, sinking his teeth and talons into his face and both sides of the neck, drawing more blood. But with another powerful blow of his trunk and two tusks, Behemoth, once again, sent Leviathan hurtling to the ground.

Job was standing precariously close to the edge of the hillside with his back facing it while still blocking all of Zerah's attacks with his sword. Job's feet slipped out from under him, and he fell backward, down over the steep embankment as his sword flew out of his hand. He rolled onto a narrow footpath, then across the width of it, and over another steep embankment. Immediately he caught hold of a tree branch. He then boosted himself back up onto the path and rested his chest and arms on it while his legs were still on the embankment. His breath came in gasps. After several seconds, he looked up to his left and saw Zerah standing on top of the hill, gazing down at him, still displaying that evil look while holding his sword high over his head. Just then, Job heard a feminine scream coming from his right. He glanced over and saw a somewhat pretty, middle-aged woman running down the embankment, onto the path, as she fled from a small avalanche of rocks caused by the battling monsters.

Up above on the plantation, Behemoth and Leviathan were still locked in mortal combat. Leviathan continued biting and tearing into Behemoth's forehead with his huge razor-sharp teeth and claws, causing more blood to flow down his face and even into his eyes. The confused and frightened Behemoth pushed forward and drove Leviathan into a huge rock pile. It collapsed over the embankment and caused an avalanche. Job and the woman looked up and saw the rocks tumbling down the hillside. Job was safely out of the path of danger to the left, and the woman only slightly to the right. She jumped behind a rock pile for safety, and Job hid his face forward in the dirt on the path. Job stayed in that position until he could hear nothing. He looked up and turned to the right and saw a second rock pile created by the avalanche between him and the rock pile the woman was hiding behind. He rose to his feet and climbed over the first rock pile, then jumped over on top of the other one, looked down, and saw the woman trapped between some rocks as both could clearly hear the roars and screams of the battling monsters above. She couldn't move to her left or she would fall over the embankment.

He asked her, "Are you all right?"

"Yes," she replied, "but I think my left ankle is broken."

He said, "You're trapped between the rocks and the hill. Don't move or you'll fall."

Job lay down forward on his chest and extended his arms down toward her. He said, "Not yet, but when I say, reach up, real fast, grab my hands. Okay, now!"

In a second, she reached up and grabbed his two hands with hers. As he pulled her up with his hands, she pushed herself up with her feet, and the ground she was standing on gave way and tumbled over the hill. As he pulled her up onto the top of the rock pile, he felt an ice-cold chill running down the back of his neck and spine that sent his flesh crawling. He stood up, turned around, and saw in front of him, on the other rock pile, Zerah, ready to slay him. Zerah rose his sword, threw it at Job, and sliced his left arm with it, causing a huge bloody gash in it. Job screamed and then grabbed hold of his arm with his right hand. Zerah held out his left arm, and the sword flew back into his hand.

Up above, Behemoth and Leviathan were still locked head-to-head, and Behemoth drove him backward to the edge of the hillside, ready to push him over. But with all his strength, Leviathan pushed himself forward, tore into Behemoth with his teeth and claws, driving him backward. The edge of the hill where the Leviathan had just pushed his hind feet into to push forward caved in, and another avalanche ensued.

Job, in a split second, turned around, threw his body on the woman, and both fell off the rock pile, onto the path. Both looked up and saw about a quarter of the embankment falling forward. Job and the woman got up and ran as fast as they could up the path, straight ahead, away from the avalanche. The tremendous rock slide struck Zerah, hurdling him the whole way down the embankment and into the valley below. After the last rock had rolled down the hill, it was quiet again. Job and the woman looked down into the valley and saw Zerah's bloody hand sticking out of the rocks, resting on the ground, still holding on to the sword.

Behemoth and Leviathan continued battling wildly and viciously. But the immense power and weight of Behemoth finally won out as he lifted Leviathan off the ground with his trunk and slammed him to the ground. Now thoroughly beaten and slain, Leviathan fell to the ground and expired. Behemoth raised his head and trunk and trumpeted a loud cry of victory over his fallen opponent.

An enraged Satan flew out of the body of Zerah high into the air directly above Job and the woman and let out an unearthly scream of anger and hatred, then darted down through the air and reentered the body of Leviathan. Job and the woman could not walk back up the hill to his plantation because much of the embankment was torn apart and covered with jagged boulders. So they walked back down onto the path. Job said, "I know another way."

They walked down the path toward the southwest, then circled around to the right, and walked up a steep hill, and came to the edge of the woods. They walked through the forest and came out where the plantation meets the woods.

As Leviathan lay motionless at the foot of the tower, the sun's rays continued to shower down upon the eyes in the face of the stone idol. The icy blue stone eyes turned from a straight-ahead position to straight down and began to melt. Both eyes turned to liquid and rained down on the top of Leviathan's corpse. The liquid turned into solid rays which struck the top of Leviathan's head. With a mighty roar, Leviathan rose back up to his feet, roared again, and fired the rays back out of his eyes, directly at Behemoth, again singeing his woolly hide. Behemoth was stunned. Again he took several steps backward. Leviathan fired the rays out of his eyes directly at Behemoth, striking him a deadly blow. Behemoth, now extremely weak, fell to his right against the statue, causing the top of it to shake and slide back and forth.

One last time, Leviathan fired a pair of rays from his eyes up into the air at Behemoth. But Behemoth was still strong enough to leap out of the way, and the rays struck the face of the stone idol. The face broke off of the head and fell to the ground. Then the entire head exploded and fell forward. The Leviathan ran forward and slammed its entire body into the tower, causing it all to fall down on top of Behemoth, knocking him to the ground.

Now, fully revived by Satan's power, Leviathan again rose to his feet and let out a cry of anger and defiance. The Behemoth rose up, too, and trumpeted a loud cry back at Leviathan to intimidate him. Leviathan was now back to full strength and more than ready for a fight, where Behemoth was totally exhausted, deeply wounded, and could never hold his own against Leviathan now. All he could do was try to intimidate and bluff his opponent with repeated roars to only indicate a challenge. But it was Satan who had possession over Leviathan, and he clearly knew the truth. Leviathan began swinging his long powerful tail, attacking Behemoth with numerous stabs in each side by the long sharp spikes that protruded from the end of it. Leviathan again bit into his face, drove his claws into his neck, and continued to stab him repeatedly with the spikes on his whiplike tail. Behemoth continued roaring and screaming in pain but still managed to put up a good fight. Now Leviathan gained the upper hand.

Job and the woman sat down on the ground at the edge of the forest. Job felt her ankle and foot. He said, "They're both hurt and swollen, but with some hot compresses, bandages, and a splint, they'll be good as new." Job tore a piece of his clothing off and bandaged her ankle. He asked, "Just who are you? Where are you from?"

She said, "My name is Dinah. And I used to live just beyond the valley there to the northeast of you. While you were gone, my husband, family, and I took your wife, Sitidos, into our care, and she lived with us. But she earned her keep. As I believe you know, she worked for us, and we paid her. But we didn't know she was already sick. She started coughing and running high fevers and, soon, she got so bad that she couldn't even get out of bed. This all came from all those damp and wet nights she had to sleep on the ground after you and her lost your home to those barbarians. We did all we could do for her. Physicians came and treated her, but she still got worse and soon died. I'm very sorry."

Job lowered his head and wept very somberly. Dinah went on, "Shortly after this, the Chaldeans invaded our home much like they did yours. They killed my whole family—my husband and five children, three sons and two daughters. They kept me as a slave to cook their meals and tend to their needs. I finally escaped from them in all this chaos. But why is all this happening? Are we going to die here like this?"

Job replied, "No! No! No! We are not going to die! I assure you! It's out of our hands now, out of our hands. Listen to me, Dinah! Put it in God's hands where it belongs!"

Dinah scoffed and said, "God? Why did he allow my husband and family to die?"

Job answered, "That's his decision to make. The Lord giveth, the Lord taketh away. Why did he allow my wife and family to be taken away from me? Maybe he has something better in store for the two of us."

While Job and Dinah were tending to each other's wounds, they heard Behemoth's scream, then a loud thump. Both looked up and saw Behemoth falling to the ground. They watched as Leviathan walked over the body of Behemoth and started walking toward them. As its body swayed from side to side like a monitor lizard, its gigantic tongue was lashing out at them, and it drew closer to them. Then they heard the same low, bloodcurdling voice coming from it that Job had heard coming from Zerah. But this time it echoed and vibrated loudly through the air and sent tremors all through Job's body as it said, "Job, Job, Job. You puny little man. Good, upright, and avoiding sin, and blameless in God's eyes. Now I'm going to devour you like the little insect that you are, you slimy little pimp. Your wife isn't even cold in her grave yet, and you got yourself another whore to do your bidding. But now, I'm finally going to devour you both. At long last, I've won!"

In an instant, its long powerful neck, lashing forked tongue, and gaping mouth reminded Job of a serpent. A serpent reminded him of the asp that killed his friend Aram, and this reminded him of the prayer that Aram gave to him and told him to say to ask for help from above during the most dire time of his life. Job thought, *This has to be the time. What could possibly be more dire than this?*

Dinah closed her eyes tightly and screamed as loud as she could, preparing herself for an agony and horror that no human being could ever imagine. Job grabbed hold of her and ran as fast as he could, deeper into the forest. Job felt the pockets in his clothing for the piece of parchment that had the prayer on it. But he couldn't find it. He hid Dinah in a patch of thick brush and said to her, "Now stay here and don't come out or even move until I say so, all right?"

"Yes," she responded.

Job ran against the trunk of a tree, and again, felt his pockets and looked in them. To his shock and horror, there was no prayer. He looked up and saw Leviathan at the edge of the forest, crashing through the trees, knocking them down while coming straight at him with its mouth partially open and saliva dripping from it. Job panicked and screamed, My God above, what will I ever do?"

Then he heard a voice from inside his head, saying, *Job, you don't need that parchment, you recited that prayer dozens of times.*

He then fell to his knees, lowered his head, and prayed these words:

> Mikhael, the archangel, defend us in battle. Be our protection against the wickedness and snares of the devil. May God rebuke him, we humbly pray. And to thou, o prince of the heavenly hosts, by the power of God, cast into hell Satan and all the other evil spirits who prowl about the world, seeking the ruin of souls. Amen.

Then the sun was darkened. At high noon, it became as dark as midnight. With a mighty earthquake and then a powerful gust of wind, the black starless sky was torn in exactly two halves. A blinding shower of light descended from the center of the gap, which gave light to the entire pitch-black countryside. This brilliant phenomenon grew increasingly smaller until it exploded outward, into a vast and spectacular burst of sparks, which then took on a single solid form. And there standing in midair was the form of a human man, of human size and stature, holding a sword above his head in his right hand with a crown on his head consisting of hundreds of golden stars and a belt around his waist, suspending a leather tartan to just above his knees. Looking up with his mouth wide open, Job uttered, "My God, it's Mikhael, the archangel! He actually exists!"

Leviathan had its head down in the trees, lashing its tongue out at Job, ready to snatch him up in his mouth. Mikhael flew overhead in a vertical position and, lowering his sword at lightning speed, sliced the back of Leviathan's neck. Again, Mikhael swung his right arm, twice this time, cutting two huge gashes through Leviathan's back armor, causing streaks of blood to appear on his flesh. The Leviathan screamed, backed out of the forest, and raised its head in the air directly in front of Mikhael. The hideous beast began roaring and snapping its enormous jaws at him. But Mikhael swung the sword, causing another deep cut in its flesh across the face; he swung it in the opposite direction again, slicing into the beast's flesh the whole way across its face. Again and again, Mikhael swung his sword, slicing into the Leviathan's neck. Mikhael plunged down through the air and swung his sword again, cutting into the soft underside of his neck, causing more streaks of blood to appear on his flesh. With another mighty roar, Leviathan backed up, inhaled and breathed out its giant flame of fire straight ahead, directly at Mikhael.

Mikhael pointed his sword toward the oncoming fire. Just as Leviathan's fire was about to strike Mikhael, a shower of bright silver sparks burst forth from the tip of the sword, then morphed into a single ball of pulsating protoplasm, creating a liquid shield, and thus protecting him from the fire. The shield absorbed and, hence, extinguished the long line of fire. Then he pulled his right arm back and hurtled the sword straight ahead. While flying straight forward through the air, it became five times larger and flew right into Leviathan's mouth. As he bit down on it, an explosion of plasma energy went all through his body, pummeling him to the ground. Now nothing but smoke poured forth from the ghastly demon's mouth as it roared in bewilderment. Mikhael rose his right hand, and the sword returned to it in its normal size.

Mikhael raised the sword above his head and lashed out again at Leviathan. He swung the sword downward, delivering a series of blows onto Leviathan's head and neck and pushing him backward. Mikhael threw his left hand into the air to distract Leviathan. As Leviathan opened its jaws and raised its head toward the hand, Mikhael swung the sword downward then upward and stabbed it into the underside of his neck. He pulled it out and stabbed it in again. As he pulled it out again, blood poured out. While being pushed backward by Mikhael, Leviathan stumbled over the carcass of Behemoth. As Mikhael sliced his sword into Leviathan's neck again, one final time, Behemoth rose to his feet. With its blood-soaked body in full view, it trumpeted its defiance and rage at Leviathan. Behemoth lowered its head almost to the ground, then raised it as fast as he could, and plunged both tusks up into the underside of Leviathan's neck. Two streams of red blood poured out onto the ground.

Behemoth pulled backward and pulled both ivory tusks out of Leviathan's neck. Leviathan screamed in pain, fell forward to the ground, and finally breathed his last. Once again, Behemoth trumpeted a mighty roar into the air and fell forward to his death, right on top of Leviathan's corpse.

As Satan departed from Leviathan's corpse, he flew straight up high into the air and let out an ear-piercing shriek. He took the form of a huge transparent gargoyle-like entity with horns sprouting from the top of its head and from the sides of its body and limbs, while enormous hooves and claws extended from both hands and feet. Two enormous black bat-like wings extended from both sides of its torso. The wings were made visible in the dark night only by countless strands of crimson veins which coursed through them, dripped with blood, and pulsated vibrantly as if they were ready to explode. He also emitted an extremely powerful stench that, to Job, smelled something like a mixture of human waste and burnt flesh. Job was so repulsed by the horrific sight and smell of the thing that he turned and lowered his head, then felt his stomach turn. He gagged twice and nearly vomited on the ground.

Standing in midair directly across from it, Mikhael pointed his sword toward the beast and emitted from the tip of it a series of silver and gold rings, which encircled the body of Satan. The rings all joined together and turned from the state of light to the state of solidity, holding Satan captive in a large transparent tube. Mikhael swung his sword to his right, sending the tube flying into the sky, over the tops of a group of mountains in the distance, then finally out of sight as a bright orange streaking trail followed behind it. And Satan was cast back into the depths of hell for disobeying God and trying to kill Job all those times when he was told not to touch him.

Again Mikhael stood in midair, this time directly above the two giant corpses and held his sword high above his right shoulder. He turned the sword in a clockwise motion as the tip of it created a bright silver circle of light in midair. He drew the sword the whole way down to the ground, causing the circle of light to extend downward until the bottom of it touched the ground, encircling both corpses in one gigantic spinning cylinder.

Mikhael then ascended high into the air above the cylinder. He pointed the sword downward toward it, and a long streak of bright gold lightning fired from the tip of it and struck the top of the cylinder. The sword and cylinder were now connected by the line of lightning between them. Mikhael held the sword tight in both hands, and in a single second, like a flash of light, he ascended high up into the air between the two halves of the severed sky and disappeared, carrying the cylinder with him in order to place the two corpses at the Lord's feet in heaven for him to do with as he will. Then the sky folded back together, and the seam left in the middle disappeared. The sun was giving her light again, and it was once again as bright as midday.

Job was sitting on a tree stump, holding his head in his hands with his elbows resting on his legs. Nearly unable to move, trembling and suffering great trauma and shock from everything that had happened to him, he kept on thinking, *My God, my God, let this all be over now and allow me to live as I used to.*

Just then, Dinah walked up behind him, placed her hands on his shoulders, and began to caress him. As they looked around, both of them saw countless sheep and cattle standing and grazing all over the plantation. The soil was rich and not charred black anymore, and all sorts of vegetation was springing up everywhere, even before their very eyes. They saw in a distance a young boy shepherding the sheep, and all the trees in the forest were lush and green once again.

Then they heard the ruffling of a bird's wings coming from above them. An extremely powerful gust of wind overcame and hurdled both of them to the ground as they watched the dirt beneath them being pushed forward by the torrential wind. They looked up and saw the Ziz flying down toward the earth, then land. The voice of the Lord came from heaven and told both of them to climb upon its back. Job took Dinah's hand and both walked upward, onto the bird's right wing, and settled on its back. The Ziz extended, then flapped its expansive wings, rose off of the ground, and flew high up into the air as Job and Dinah both felt the wind blowing through their hair and watched the trees below them bending over from the force of the gales caused by the flapping of the bird's wings.

The great Ziz flew over the lake, carrying Job and Dinah toward the castle nestled on the high mountainside. The Ziz perched its feet on the top of a mountain above the castle and extended its left wing downward, right in front of the front castle door. Job and Dinah climbed off the bird's back, then down the wing, and were standing in front of the castle door. Everything looked as if nothing had ever happened. Job was so overjoyed to see and know that he had all of this back again and that the castle looked like it had never been touched.

The Lord spoke to Job, saying, "Though you angered me many times with your words of ignorance and arrogance, you still never cursed me, and you held your faith well during all you endured. And because you have resisted all temptation and, again, you never cursed me, not even once, and you did not listen to your wife, I forgive all of your words and misdeeds. As you can see, I have now restored everything to you that you once owned, and you shall never be troubled again."

And after the Lord had spoken these words to Job, he said to Eliphaz the Temanite, "My anger blazes against you and your two friends! You have not spoken rightly about me, as has my servant Job. So now take seven bulls and seven rams and go to my servant Job and sacrifice a burnt offering for yourselves, and let my servant, Job, pray for you. To him I will show favor and not punish your folly, for you have not spoken rightly concerning me, as has my servant, Job."

Then Eliphaz, Bildad the Shuhite, and Zophar the Naamathite went and did as the Lord had commanded them. Then the Lord showed favor to Job. In his ecstatic joy, Job fell to his knees and fervently prayed to the Lord, giving him thanks for restoring to him all he had lost, and asking him to forgive his three friends.

The Lord also restored the prosperity of Job after he had prayed for his friends; the Lord finally forgave the three of them, showed favor to them, and sent them on their way home. The Lord even gave Job twice as much as he had before. Then all his brothers and sisters came to him, as well as all his former acquaintances, and they dined with him in his castle. They consoled and comforted him for all the evil the Lord had allowed to be wrought upon him, and each one gave him a piece of money and a gold ring.

Thus the Lord blessed the later days of Job more than his earlier ones. Now he had fourteen thousand sheep, six thousand camels, a thousand yoke of oxen, and a thousand she-donkeys. He also had seven sons and three daughters: the first daughter he called Jemimah, the second, Keziah, and the third, Keren-happuch. In all the land, no other women were as beautiful as the daughters of Job, and their father gave them an inheritance among their brothers.

After this, Job lived a hundred and forty years; and he saw his children, his grandchildren, and even his great-grandchildren. Then Job died, old and full of years and prosperity.

And after Job and the last of his descendants were all taken into heaven, all the angels and members of the divine council could plainly see a large white cloud above the castle with the Lord's right hand extending out of it, holding Job, Dinah, and all of their ancestors and descendants. And all these heavenly hosts worshipped and sang thanks and praise to the Lord in these words, "And he will raise you up on eagles' wings and hold you in the palm of his hand."

ABOUT THE AUTHOR

James Yeager has been a lifelong devotee of movies, literature, and the Bible for most of his life. His favorite film genres are biblical epics, sci-fi, action, and western films. In this one book, he pays tribute to all of these great genres. For his senior seminar at the University of Pittsburgh, where he majored in communications and theater, he wrote a forty-page essay on how science fiction films of the 1950s reflected society's greatest fears of the time.

After graduation in 1989, he worked for two local radio stations. Power 92 was the first where he mainly worked in the traffic department and wrote commercials for the station's sponsors. The second was WADJ in Somerset, Pennsylvania, where he worked as a disc jockey and announced upcoming sports events, weather, and news. Currently, Jim lives in Harrisburg, Pennsylvania. He works for the commonwealth and attends Holy Name of Jesus Church every weekend.

www.ingramcontent.com/pod-product-compliance
Lightning Source LLC
Chambersburg PA
CBHW021117130726
47988CB00003B/1054